T0142767

Individualized Service Plans

Empowering People with Disabilities

By

Paul Spicer, QMRP

Founder and President of Spicer & Associates, LLC
www.spicerassociates.com

authorHOUSE®

AuthorHouse™
1663 Liberty Drive
Bloomington, IN 47403
www.authorhouse.com
Phone: 1 (800) 839-8640

© 2005 Paul Spicer, QMRP. All Rights Reserved.

No part of this book may be reproduced, stored in a retrieval system, or transmitted by any means without the written permission of the author.

Published by AuthorHouse 08/15/2018

ISBN: 978-1-4208-2274-8 (sc)

Print information available on the last page.

Any people depicted in stock imagery provided by Getty Images are models, and such images are being used for illustrative purposes only.
Certain stock imagery © Getty Images.

This book is printed on acid-free paper.

Because of the dynamic nature of the Internet, any web addresses or links contained in this book may have changed since publication and may no longer be valid. The views expressed in this work are solely those of the author and do not necessarily reflect the views of the publisher, and the publisher hereby disclaims any responsibility for them.

"…The problem arises when services take over the life of someone they're supposed to be supporting. When this happens, people and their families lose the freedom to control their lives – even lose the basic belief in their ability to do so. They also lose the relationships with other human beings that are basic building blocks of life. Instead they become surrounded by people who are paid to be with them, to organize, manage, direct and oversee their lives. At that point the social service system assumes a measure of control that most of the rest of us would find intolerable and it isolates them from other people outside the system, from the community…"

(Taken from The Gift of Hospitality, By Mary O'Connell, 1988)

TABLE OF CONTENTS

INDIVIDUALIZED SERVICE PLANS

INTRODUCTION

Have you ever stared deeply into a lushly landscaped Japanese fishpond and wondered about the oversized goldfish swimming peacefully below? These brightly colored fish are called Koi and have an interesting relationship to their surrounding. If a Koi is kept in a small fish bowl it will not grow significantly. However, placed in a large pond the Koi will begin to grow in striking proportions. Free a Koi in an even larger natural lake and it can really stretch out and reach its full potential. In fact, the average Koi can grow to 24 to 36 inches if given the right sized pond and proper aeration.

Psychologists and sociologists have often used this relationship, coined the "Koi Phenomenon, to describe the relationship human beings have with their own surroundings. Not surprising, is the fact that many individuals with disabilities have related this analogy to the achievements, and set backs, they have experienced when dealing with the world in which they live. In recent years, individuals with mental retardation and developmental disabilities, who were living isolated in segregated institutions, are now moving to community-based homes. With this move towards community integration it becomes obvious that individuals with disabilities can overreach previously conceived limitations when allowed the opportunity to experience true growth.

Moving into a new era marked with, slow but steady, improvement for people with mental retardation we see the lesson in the Koi phenomenon. A person's true potential can only be developed when given the opportunity to grow in a natural and nonrestrictive environment. With this changing landscape of our community we all must find new ways to integrate individuals of all ability levels into life. There is an increasing need for articles, publications, and course books designed to assist instructors, caregivers, family members, and educators in the effort to better implement techniques that encourage special populations to maximize their potential.

This publication provides a format for individuals wishing to learn more about designing fully inclusive services for individuals with disabilities. The following materials have been gathered using an interdisciplinary team of case managers, QMRPs, training specialists, recreational therapists, behavioral management consultants, and policy makers – all wishing to improve the service system, and thus the lives, of individuals with disabilities.

INDIVIDUALIZED SERVICE PLANS

A WORD OF CAUTION

Before you begin, it is crucial to consider the multiple aspects that make up one's unique personal characteristics. For this reason, no single book or learning resource (no matter how comprehensive) can capture the array of attributes of any one human being. Healthcare providers and therapists are cautioned to use the following materials as a resource and not as a "one size fits all" approach to caregiving.

The bulk of this publication is comprised of pre written goals and objectives that have been successfully utilized by service systems from around the United States. The provided examples are just that – examples. It would be insulting to say that a packaged, or canned approach, to the delivery of services would touch upon all the various aspects of a client's life. Thus, it goes without saying – your client's personal choice, individual interests, and vision for the future should always be taken into consideration first.

Disclaimer:

Creating an individualized service plan for individuals with disabilities is often required for agency staff who provide Medicaid-reimbursed Residential Support, Personal Assistance, Day Support, In Home Care, or Prevocational services. In addition, various other funding sources and accrediting boards, such as Commission on Accreditation of Rehabilitation Facilities (CARF), require a clear plan of action that is person centered. It is a necessity that all healthcare providers possess basic proficiency and competency as identified by their own state and/or governing board. This publication does not purport to outline the guidelines of any one state or governing body.

SECTION ONE

10 Steps to Writing Effective Service Plans

INDIVIDUALIZED SERVICE PLANS

STEP ONE: Defining Ability

All healthcare providers must first possess basic proficiency and competency before beginning to develop a plan of care for individuals with disabilities. The first step in becoming a proficient leader in your chosen field is to understand the definitions commonly utilized in helping relations.

True human growth, for individuals of all ability levels, must occur in a natural environment. However, even with the advancements made there is a tendency to create separate programs and artificial environments for individuals with developmental disabilities. Thus, it is extremely important for society as a whole to understand that a developmental disability is merely based on not achieving certain developmental milestones of functioning by a certain age and does not warrant any form of segregation. Developmental disabilities are varied and can include mental retardation, cerebral palsy, spinal bifida, autism, epilepsy, and specific learning disabilities. The label does not mean that the person is incapable of living, working, and participating in life with the proper support system.

According to the American Association on Mental Retardation, there are three characteristics that must be present to meet the definition of mental retardation.

- <u>Significantly sub average general intellectual functioning</u> – an IQ score of approximately 70 to 75 or below based on individually administered intelligence tests.

- <u>Significant limitations in adaptive skills in two or more of the following areas</u>: communication, self care, home living, social skills, community use, self direction, health and safety, functional academics, leisure and work.

- <u>Appears before age of 18</u>.

Your Role:

Age-Appropriate Activities

Unfortunately, individuals with developmental disabilities are already at risk of being stigmatized or misunderstood. For this reason, one should always be mindful of teaching methods that may make a person with a disability look childish or different. All lesson plans, activities, and events involving persons with disabilities should be age-appropriate in nature. Encourage individuals with disabilities to participate in activities that are carried out exactly the same, or as closely possible, as that of a person without a disability. Do not use childlike toys, games, or teaching tools. As a caregiver, understand that your interactions and teaching practices effect the public perception towards persons with disabilities.

Normalization

Too often health care providers and caregivers are quick to overcompensate for a person with a disability by creating specialized classes, events, and unnatural learning environments. Instead, learning should take place through natural opportunities and in real situations. The principle of normalization centers on the fact that individuals with disabilities should be encouraged to live lives that are just like those of peers in the community.

For example, caregivers should encourage individuals with disabilities to buy attractive and well fitting clothing, obtain attractive and normal haircuts, select homes or group homes among everyday neighborhoods, and access age appropriate social outlets. It is also important to remember that individuals with developmental disabilities may at times have difficulty transferring skills from one activity or environment to another. Therefore, activities should be arranged to take place within the natural environment to eliminate potential transference barriers. In closing, health care providers should maintain the same rules, strategies, and steps as for a person without a disability whenever possible.

Least Intrusive Measures

Training and assisting an individual with a disability should always be implemented in a fashion that is respectful and delivered in the least intrusive fashion to meet the person's preferences. Often people will attempt to do too much, speak with a loud tone of voice, or exaggerate facial expression when working with an individual with a disability. As with interacting with any individual, it is always best to determine what perimeters and teaching techniques are most acceptable to the person. Once these perimeters have been established, it is important to provide the least amount of support needed for the person to still be successful. Always allow for personal growth and independence. Begin to fade out of the picture, by providing less prompting, as the person begins to grasp the skill.

Dignity of Risk

All people, with or without a disability, should be given the chance to take risks that are typical with ordinary life. In this way, individuals are allowed to experience true growth and development when not overly protected. Placing individuals with disabilities into large institutions, or other sheltering techniques, is interfering with the ability to experience the same livelihood as other people. Caregivers should encourage clients to develop informed decision making skills so that to make individualized decisions. For example, individuals with disabilities should be encouraged to get jobs, access public transportation, go on dates, become volunteers, and participate in recreational/sporting activities.

Natural Support

Individuals with disabilities are often inundated with support from paid staff members and caregivers without making use of supports that are naturally available in the community. Family, friends, neighbors, classmates, and co-workers can often help to reinforce skills better than a trained professional. Caregivers should assist individuals with disabilities in conversation and socialization skills so that friendships can be made with other friends, classmates, and peers outside the disability service system. Recruiting volunteers, promoting the "buddy system," and pairing up individuals with similar interests can promote this process. Observing and encouraging the natural bonds occurring between a person with a disability and a new acquaintance can also help in the creation of natural supports.

Accommodations

A good healthcare provider has the ability to work around a client's weaknesses by finding different ways to perform a difficult task. In such a case, the learning environment and the task at hand must be closely observed for potential accommodations. Once a problematic area, for example a reading problem or inability to screen out extraneous stimuli, has been identified it is possible to develop accommodations that compensate for the deficit. Consider all factors involved in the task to find the specific problematic area. Perform a task analysis by breaking the skill down to each basic step. Consider assistive devices, technology, or homemade devices such as pictures, symbolic reminders, and color codes.

Paul Spicer, QMRP

People First Language

Referring to a person as "handicapped," "retarded," and "crippled" perpetuates society's myths about people with disabilities and fosters a stereotypical perception. Thus a person should always be defined as a person first, instead of as a disability. Realize and understand that a disability is merely a body function that operates differently and should therefore not define a person. Refrain from the use of labels. The only labels required in addressing a person with a disability is by their birth name. Lastly, remember that a disability is simply a medical diagnosis not what a person is. Someone with mental retardation is not "retarded" but rather a "person with a disability."

Human Rights

Most importantly, all healthcare providers and caregivers must understand that individuals with disabilities have the same human rights as non-disabled people. Some individuals with disabilities may have had their legal rights limited through the appointment of a guardian or another legal process. However, it is mandatory that providers not attempt to unfairly limit or place restrictions on managing money, voting, shopping, etc. We are all entitled to the same rights – such as free speech, voting, marrying, and privacy. As a healthcare provider it is your duty to be aware of all of these rights. Reviewing these rights with your clients is extremely important and should be at the forefront of your mind.

TEST YOUR KNOWLEDGE:

I. TRUE AND FALSE

1) True/False	A person with a developmental disability does not achieve certain developmental milestones of functioning by a certain age.
2) True/False	Life goals will always take a person with a disability exactly ten years to accomplish.
3) True/False	The goal of a caregiver working with an individual with a developmental disability should be to fix the person to be more like an able bodied individual.
4) True/False	Developing care plans in an "age appropriate" manner consist of refraining from the use of childlike teaching methods by creating an adult learning environment.
5) True/False	Healthcare providers should always look for opportunities to create segregated and specialized classes for individuals with developmental disabilities.
6) True/False	When assisting an individual with a developmental disability it is important to use the same rules, strategies, and steps as for a person without a disability whenever possible.
7) True/False	Rewarding an individual with food is an appropriate method of reducing or decreasing a specific behavior through reinforcement.
8) True/False	The manner in which a caregiver interacts with an individual with a developmental disability tells the person, and the public, a lot about how the instructor views that person.
9) True/False	Individuals with mental retardation and other developmental disabilities do not have the same basic rights as those without disabilities.
10) True/False	An example of using "natural supports" is helping a person with a disability to join the neighborhood association where they live, so they can meet some of their neighbors.

Answer Key: 1) T 2) F 3) F 4) T 5) F 6) T 7) F 8) T 9) F 10) T

Paul Spicer, QMRP

II. MULTIPILE CHOICE

1) *Persons with mental retardation:*

   A) Are all very similar

   B) Always need assistance with personal hygiene

   C) Are all very different individuals

   D) All of the above

2) *A person with a developmental disability should be referred to as:*

   A) "Retarded"

   B) "Handicapped"

   C) A person first, instead of as a disability

   D) None of the above

3) *One of the most important staff responsibilities in following the concept of "dignity of risk" is:*

   A) Allowing the people you support to do anything they choose to do.

   B) Telling the people you support what you think is the safest way for them to behave.

   C) Suggest to the individual that "real life" is too hard and a segregated "special" environment may be more appropriate.

   D) Providing the people you support with meaningful information about the possible consequences of their actions so they can make informed choices.

Multiple Choice Answer Key:

   1) C

   2) C

   3) D

III.SHORT ANSWER

1) Describe the importance of creating accommodations for individuals with disabilities in the natural environment.

2) List three manners in which a caregiver can better involve a person with a disability into their natural environment.

Answer Key:

1) *As a caregiver or healthcare provider it is your responsibility to closely examine the person, the learning environment, and the task at hand. A good provider will identify and work around the person's weaknesses so that to fully participate in community life. Working around a problematic area may at times require the use of accommodations. Accommodations may include assistive devices, technology, or homemade visual aides. By creating accommodations that break the problematic area down to more manageable and achievable steps the caregiver has increased the likelihood of full community participation and success.*

2) A caregiver or healthcare provider wishing to better involve a person with a disability into a more inclusive environment should first seek out the person's desires, interests, and vision for the experience. Once a mutually acceptable plan of action has been reached the caregiver should examine the learning environment so that to eliminate distractions and identify problematic areas. As the assistance process develops the caregiver should encourage the use of "natural supports" that are available in the community. Seek out flexible ways of providing services in the community setting that emphasizes supports that are naturally available - family, friends, co-workers, and neighbors. In the same manner, identify training areas that are available in an everyday community setting – grocery stores, laundromats, city bus systems, etc.

Paul Spicer, QMRP

IV. SHORT ESSAY

Kelly is a 25-year-old female diagnosed with mild mental retardation. Kelly lives on her own with assistance from a case manager and social worker. Her home is situated in a small subdivision within walking distance of an exercise gym, shopping mall, community center, and swimming pool. However, Kelly chooses to watch TV by herself in her spare time and is not generally encouraged by others to explore additional social, recreational, or sporting activities. Kelly is becoming increasingly overweight but does not exhibit any other abnormal physical symptoms at this time that would limit her from engaging in an exercise routine. Kelly feels isolated and would like to improve her mental and physical well being.

Describe the steps you would take as a health professional to involve Kelly in a community based routine while implementing a healthy lifestyle.

Answer Key:

Despite having a developmental disability Kelly is very capable of living a productive livelihood in a community environment. She is fortunate to live in an area within walking distance of many recreational options and have the support of a social worker. However, Kelly is not fully accessing the resources available to her as evidenced by her limited network of natural supports and friends, lack of recreational and social interests, and declining physical health.

Kelly would benefit from a wide array of recreational opportunities offered at the local gym and community center in her neighborhood. Kelly should be encouraged to join the gym and to explore the many classes offered by trained healthcare professionals. Upon joining the gym, and before beginning any physical fitness training, she should consult her primary care physician for a functionally graded exercise test, body fat assessment, and heart rate assessment/blood pressure measurements.

Healthcare professionals working with Kelly in the local gym and in the community center should offer the same recreational options available to Kelly as they would to an individual without a disability. Kelly should be encouraged to join the classes she is interested in learning about and participate in the level of training she feels best suits her needs. In addition, Kelly should be encouraged to socialize and network with other individuals in the community to develop natural friendships and supports.

Kelly's success in accessing and utilizing these resources is highly dependent on the accommodations put into place by instructors and healthcare providers. At the root of all assistance should be the mindset of respect and equal community partnership. Kelly's network of supports should not attempt to "fix" her to be like an able-bodied individual but rather empower her by celebrating her diversity and unique talents. When and if a problematic area does arise the healthcare worker should seek out ways to identify the root of the difficulty and implement suitable accommodations for her full participation. Effective teaching practices such as age appropriate instruction, eliminating distraction, the use of concrete language, and "show, opposed to tell" methods should all be utilized for maximum success.

INDIVIDUALIZED SERVICE PLANS

STEP TWO: Person Centered Planning

"Chesire Puss…would you tell me, please, which way I ought to go from here?"

"That depends a good deal on where you want to get to, " said the Cat.

"I don't much care where -," said Alice.

"Then it doesn't much matter which way you go," said the Cat.

Lewis Carroll
Alice's Adventure in Wonderland

Paul Spicer, QMRP

From Medicaid to CARF, no matter the funding or governing source, all providers should encourage personal choice. By doing so, individuals with disabilities may define and express their individual identity:

Creating a plan of care involves many steps, however none so important as developing an atmosphere of personal choice. Providers in charge of writing a plan of care (often referred to as an individualized service plan or client service plan) need to understand the value of autonomy in everyday matters. In this manner, the plan of care should emphasize opportunities to make both small everyday decision and large life defining decisions. In the end, the service plan should be based on the individual's abilities, needs, interests, and vision for the future.

If an individual tells you – by words or behaviors – that their ultimate goal in life is to drive across country in a rented Volkswagen Beatle, then it's your responsibility to become a "roadblock remover." No matter how outrageous the goal, the client's voice should be heard and respected. Maybe the person will never have a chance to realize their cross-country dream. However, you should encourage that person to start talking about possible ways to come close to the goal.

Suggest a driving simulator at a local mall, explore possible road trips with a companion, or study a DMV manual. Better yet, attempt to figure out what the person really wants out of the identification of a specific goal. Is the person wanting to learn to drive, or really seeking freedom, independence, and the feeling of adulthood? Whatever the case may be, take each person's goal seriously.

Improving upon the delivery of services for people with disabilities involves examining the very foundation of each individual's plan of care. At the root of all plans should be the mindset of respect and equal community partnership. It is therefore crucial that the goal in writing a plan of care is never to fix a person to be like an able bodied individual, but rather to empower a person by celebrating their own diversity and unique talents. In the end, the person's plan and the way the program operates should be based on the individual's needs, interests, and desires.

On the following pages, you'll learn the elements that are crucial when developing a person centered plan of care....

BEFORE YOU BEGIN

Good healthcare providers make it a point to use a variety tools, techniques, and methods to encourage client participation. Consider the following examples to prompt your client to participate fully in the development of their own plan of care.

Sometimes a formalized worksheet can encourage clients to think about the needs, desires, and vision for the future. Including such a form in a service plan or reviewing it at a client meeting can help facilitate the creation of a plan of care. If a client cannot fill out such a form on their own, then fill in their exact comments and thoughts using quotations.

Example 1:

PERSON CENTERED PLANNING WORKSHEET

THINGS THAT WORK FOR ME (Record topics that *make you happy*, successful, and motivated)	THINGS THAT DON"T WORK FOR ME (Record topics that *make you unhappy*, unsuccessful, and lead to failure)
Example Answer: Positive people, humor, and an energetic approach.	*Example Answer:* Negative people and comments.
Example Answer: Being treated like an adult, being treated like I don't have a disability.	*Example Answer:* Being treated "like a baby."
Example Answer: Music – especially classic rock and guitars. However, a fan of all kinds of music.	*Example Answer:* Being "nagged" or spoken to in an authoritative manner
Example Answer: Redskins football, college football, baseball	*Example Answer:* Being touched or hugged first (likes to be the first to initiate touch).
Example Answer: Special Olympics Sporting Events- basketball and softball.	*Example Answer:* Having my routine being disrupted.

Paul Spicer, QMRP

<u>Example 2</u>:

Personal Inventory

What Works What makes you happy/successful? What is enjoyable to you; calms you?	What Does Not Work What makes you feel unsuccessful; unhappy, worse if you're upset?
Jane Smith is very enthusiastic about trying new things, learning new facts, and keeping up with current events. She holds a number of hobbies and favorite past times. For instance, she is a "movie buff" and enjoys watching and talking about Walt Disney films. Jane's most favorite travel destinations are Disney World, the State Fair, and the beach. In addition to travel Jane is a "food fanatic" and enjoys tasting new foods and trying new restaurants. Jane likes and thrives off of a structured routine. She has a pattern in which she likes her day to follow. Jane enjoys a positive approach and reacts best with peers and staff who utilize a positive/humorous communication style.	Jane Smith has a difficult time controlling her anger, stress, and level of agitation. Jane dislikes being told what to do and she states, "I don't like being talked to like a baby." She often is overheard stating "I don't like being ordered around" and "you don't know who you're talking to." Often Jane misperceives other's communication style and makes inappropriate comments as a result. Jane has extreme difficulty in pronouncing words. She gets agitated when others do not understand what she is attempting to say or when a person pretends to understand what she is saying

Gifts and Attributes What do people who know and care about you think/say? (Special skills/ talents)	Barriers to Acceptance What gets in the way of people knowing and caring about you?
Jane is motivated to learn new things and is often much more up to date and informed of matters, current events, and facts than most people give her credit. Jane is a trivia and movie buff and can speak on a wide range of subjects. Unfortunately, many people do not give her the time to communicate her message or have the ability to understand her speech. When her speech is understood other people are surprised to learn that she has a wonderful sense of humor and grasp on her surroundings. Jane is very active in her church as well as the Hanover ARC, Special Olympics, and Hanover Parks and Recreation. She is very driven to try new things and actively participates in various social and recreational outlets.	Jane has a history of seizure disorder and takes medication for seizure control. Jane has mild hearing loss in one ear and often does not hear others talking to her. Jane's physician has recommend that she limit her intake of products high in caffeine and sugar. Jane is easily agitated and should be encouraged to routinely apply stress/anger management techniques.

INDIVIDUALIZED SERVICE PLANS

STEP THREE: Utilizing A Functional Assessment

The key to developing a quality plan of care is to balance the client's individual interests with their support needs.

Once you've developed an understanding of the client's unique hobbies and interests, you must utilize an assessment tool to grasp the level of support needed to assist the client in accessing these interests.

Most service providers are required to use a formal assessment tool to gather information to determine their client's current level of needed support. The best way to learn about a client, and any person for that matter, is to spend time with them in as many different settings as possible. In this way you'll get a first hand perspective on what they can and cannot do, what they like and dislike, and what supports are required. The information gathered can then be recorded using an assessment tool – generally containing checklists, commentary, and functional skills assessments.

The importance of functional assessment tools must not be overlooked. However, even more important is the ability to understand the results of the assessment and how it relates to an individual. In the end the tool is not only implemented to shed light on what the client cannot, but more importantly what they can do. In this way the emphasis is in creating the plan of care is focused on identifying an individual's strengths and interests and building upon them.

Things to Consider When Developing or Implementing a Functional Assessment:

- Individuals with disabilities often communicate through behaviors when they are unable to talk or understand spoken language. A functional assessment and summary of an individual's abilities should therefore include both verbal and behavioral cues.

- Respect all individuals when performing an assessment. Testing makes some people nervous and act in an unusual manner.

- Utilize multiple environments, with emphasis placed on the most natural settings.

- Think about how you would feel if you were asked numerous questions about personal matters and were scored on your ability to address daily tasks.

- Understand that the behaviors you observe are at times an individual's way of controlling and directing their own lives.

- Don't get caught up in the level of disability, what services the person has received in the past, or what other psychologists and physicians may recommend.

- Make sure the assessment is functional in nature – representing the individual's strengths, interests, and support needs.

Review the functional assessment provided on the next several pages to familiarize yourself with what kinds of questions are crucial in developing a plan of care that recognizes the individual's support needs.

Example:

FUNCTIONAL ASSESSMENT

Ability to Access Community Resources	Never	Sometimes	Often	Comments
Demonstrates the ability to use telephone independently:				
A. Locates numbers in the telephone directory (specify residential, business, blue and yellow pages).				
B. Locates addresses in telephone directory.				
C. Dials numbers presented orally.				
D. Dials written numbers.				
E. Can obtain telephone assistance in an emergency (911)				
F. Can use directory assistance (411)				
G. Can make purchases utilizing vending machine				
H. Can select/order items for purchase				
I. Can order a meal				
J. Can identify sight words				
K. Can pay bus/train fare				
L. Can recognize and get off at the correct stop				
M. Can read bus schedules				
N. Can identify community signs				
O. Stops at curb				
P. Looks both ways before crossing				
Q. Can identify community safety signs				

Learning and Problem Solving	Never	Sometimes	Often	Comments
Time Management/Can use clock to manage time:				
A. Tells time to the minute				
B. Tells time to the quarter hour				
C. Tells time to the half hour				
D. Tells time to the hour				
E. Matches activities to time (lunch-12:00; leave-3:00)				
1. Can read a calendar				
Money Management				
A. Sort/Match coins				
B. Can maintain a checking account				
C. Can write checks				
D. Can shop comparatively for groceries				
E. Can budget expenses (weekly, monthly)				
F. Can add prices of 3-5 items				
G. Can use a calculator				
H. Can write dollars and cents in decimal notation				
I. Can read dollars and cents in decimal notation				
J. Can count various coin and bill combinations				
K. Can identify bill denominations				
L. Can count coin combinations up to $1.00				
M. States the value of each coin				
N. Can identify coins by name				
O. Demonstrates understanding of more or less				
P. Can prepare a menu/food groups				
Q. Can prepare a grocery list				

R. Can count objects (1-?)				
S. Can recognize numbers				
T. Identifies appropriate tool/utensil for specific task				
U. Identifies appropriate cleanser/ chemical for specific task				

Personal Care & Hygiene	Never	Sometimes	Often	Comments
Eating:				
1. Is able to feed self without assistance.				
2. Cuts food with a knife instead of eating pieces, which are too large.				
3. Feeds self with a fork.				
4. Feeds self with a spoon.				
5. Feeds self with hands.				
Demonstrates ability to eat:				
A. Solid foods				
B. Semi-solid				
C. Liquids				
1. Takes small bites and chews food slowly.				
2. Chews food thoroughly with mouth closed.				
3. Drinks from a cup without spilling.				
4. Drinks from a cup with assistance.				
5. Drinks from a straw.				

Toileting	Never	Sometimes	Often	Comments
1. Independently cares for all toileting needs without being minded and without assistance.				
2. Cares for all toileting needs with prompting.				

3. Fastens and adjusts clothing after toileting.				
A. Zips zippers				
B. Buttons large buttons				
C. Buttons small buttons				
D. Fasten snaps				
4. Can put on and remove elastic waist garments.				
5. Pulls down pants when preparing to use the toilet.				
6. Pulls up pants when toileting is completed.				
7. Asks to use toilet (verbalizing, gestures).				
8. Needs a toileting schedule.				
9. Wears Depends.				
10. Indicates wet or soiled pants by vocalizing or gesturing.				
11. Can put on and remove front opening of coat and/or sweater.				

Hygiene	Never	Sometimes	Often	Comments
1. Washes and dries hands without assistance.				
2. Demonstrates appropriate health care skills (uses tissue to blow nose, covers mouth when sneezes/coughs-washes hands afterwards, etc.)				
3. Demonstrates appropriate hygiene skills (reports to program clean and free of offensive odor)				
4. Grooms hair and nails appropriately.				
5. Can brush teeth without being reminded and without assistance.				

Endurance	Never	Sometimes	Often	Comments
1. Absences do not exceed 1 day per month.				
Remains on a specific task for extended periods of time:				
A. Alone (how long?)				
B. With others (how long?)				
2. Demonstrates ability to stand/walk for up to 4 hours.				
3. Demonstrates ability to lift, push and pull items.				

Gross Motor	Never	Sometimes	Often	Comments
1. Walks up and down stairs without assistance.				
2. Runs without falling				
3. Walks as a primary means of getting around.				
4. Walks across a room without assistance.				
5. Takes at least two steps without assistance.				
6. Walks when holding a stable object (i.e.-handrails, tables, walls, etc.)				
7. Pulls self to a standing position.				
Is independently mobile with the use of:				
A. Walker				
B. Wheelchair				
8. Is able to sit unsupported.				
9. Holds head erect without assistance.				

Fine Motor Skills	Never	Sometimes	Often	Comments
Cuts with scissors:				
A. Complex items				
B. Simple geometric shapes				
C. Along a straight line				
D. Across a piece of paper				
1. Opens doors by turning and pulling doorknobs.				
2. Opens doors that require only pushing or pulling.				

Fine Motor Skills Cont.-	Never	Sometimes	Often	Comments
3. Copies letters, numbers and shapes.				
4. Traces letters, numbers and shapes.				
5. Holds pencil in proper position for writing.				
6. Marks with pencil, crayon or chalk.				
7. Picks up small objects with thumb and forefinger.				
8. Picks up small objects with hands.				
9. Unwraps small objects like gum or candy.				
10. Puts objects into small containers and takes them out again.				
11. Transfers objects from one hand to another.				
12. Voluntarily grasps and holds objects.				
13. Controls release of objects.				
14. Demonstrates strong fine motor skills				

Communication	Never	Sometimes	Often	Comments
Communicates basic needs through verbal expression:				
A. Speaks in 3-4 word phrases.				
B. Speaks in complete sentences.				
C. Communicates thoughts and feelings.				
D. Has difficulty pronouncing words, speaking clearly.				
E. Communicates basic needs through signs/gestures.				
Follows Instructions:				
A. Five steps and more				
B. Three to four steps				
C. One to two steps				
Demonstrates understanding of instructions including:				
A. In/On/Beside				
B. Right/Left				
C. Under/Over				
D. Yes/No				
1. Initiates contact with staff when instructions are not understood.				
2. Responds immediately to safety commands/signals.				
3. Maintains eye contact during conversations.				
4. Responds when spoken to or name is called (vocalizes or turns to speaker).				
Communicates primarily by means of:				
A. Verbal expression				
B. Finger spelling				
C. Signs				
D. Gestures				
E. Communication book/board				

5. Communicates loudly enough to be heard/understood.				
Communicates the following basic needs:				
A. Thirst				
B. Hunger				
C. Pain				
D. Sickness				
E. Toileting needs				
6. Communicates wants and desires				

Socialization	Never	Sometimes	Often	Comments
1. Initiates conversation with others.				
2. Relates appropriately with peers (treats others with respect).				
3. Assists peers/complies with requests from peers.				
4. Greets others and/or introduces self appropriately.				
5. Plays a variety of games (simple, complex-keeps score).				
6. Waits turn while engaged in activity.				
7. Responds to sensory stimuli.				
8. Addresses at least two familiar people by name.				
9. Plays more than one board or card game requiring making decisions, keeping score and/or based on chance.				
10. Can wait his/her turn while playing games.				
11. Plays simple group games in which someone wins, but score is not kept.				

Personal Awareness	Never	Sometimes	Often	Comments
1. Completes detailed forms (job/credit applications, etc.)				
2. Completes forms using basic personal information				
3. Can write and state social security number				
4. Can write and state home address				
5. Can write and state home phone number				
6. Can write and state date of birth.				
7. Can write name using cursive notation.				
8. Can write (print) and state first and last name				
9. Can print first name				
10. Can recognize name when written				
11. Presents I.D. card upon request				

Behavior	Never	Sometimes	Often	Comments
Demonstrates behavior that interferes with the safety of self and/or others.				
A. Physical aggression				
B. Verbal aggression				
C. Self-abuse				
D. Inappropriate sexual behavior				
1. Remains with a group or assigned area.				
Demonstrates respect for property:				
A. Destroys property				
B. Takes property that belongs to someone else				
2. Complies with staff requests				

Paul Spicer, QMRP

3. Independently weighs consequences of actions before making decisions				
4. Demonstrates self-control				
5. Shows an excessive or peculiar preoccupation with objects or activities.				
6. Displays repetitive behaviors (i.e., rocking, pacing, etc.)				
Can remain focused on a specific activity for:				
A. Extended periods of time.				
B. 30 minutes				
C. 15 minutes				
D. 10 minutes				
E. 5 minutes or less				
7. Can remain focused on specific activity with others for an allotted amount of time.				
8. Complies with staff request				
9. Respects property of others (not taking items belonging to others)				
10. Eats or puts non-edible items in mouth (PICA).				

Safety/Health	Never	Sometimes	Often	Comments
1. Demonstrates appropriate food handling skills.				
2. Demonstrates basic safety skills (i.e., does not touch hot surfaces, uses caution with wet floor, handles knives correctly, does not mix cleaning chemicals, does not pick up broken glass with hands, etc.)				
3. Demonstrates ability to determine freshness/spoilage of food.				
4. Demonstrates knowledge of proper food storage.				

5. Demonstrates ability to use basic appliances.				
6. Identifies and understands basic safety signs such as: caution, danger, poison, exit, wet floor, warning, emergency.				
7. Identifies emergency from non-emergency situations.				

Paul Spicer, QMRP

PUTTING IT ALL TOGETHER

Below you will find an example summary written by a social worker attempting to create a plan of care for their client. The social worker has taken the time to observe the client in natural settings and everyday environments. Through this interaction the social worker has been able to obtain the client's interests and vision for the future. A functional assessment tool has been utilized to gain a better understanding of the client's support needs. Now the social worker must summarize the accumulated information before writing the actual plan of care.

Below you will find an example of this summary.

Example: FUNCTIONAL ASSESMENT SUMMARY

FUNCTIONAL ASSESSMENT SUMMARY

Likes	Jane is very enthusiastic about trying new things, learning new facts, and keeping up with current events. Because of this interest she holds a number of hobbies and favorite past times. Jane is very interested in traveling and tourist destinations. Jane often carries with her souvenirs, maps, and reminders of her most recent vacations. She collects, and proudly displays, these items in her room at home as well. In addition to travel Jane enjoys tasting new foods and trying new restaurants. Jane often proclaims, "anything new is what I want." Jane's most favorite activity is planning lunch outings with friends and staff members. In addition to the many hobbies listed above, Jane likes and thrives off of a structured routine. She has a pattern in which she likes her day to follow and dislikes disruptions. Jane also enjoys a positive approach and a sense of humor. She often misperceives others as threatening in voice tone and body language. In this manner she reacts best and builds rapport with peers and staff who utilize a positive and humorous communication style. Jane has extreme difficulty in pronouncing words and thus communicating her feelings. Jane likes it when others repeat what she has said so that she knows they are aware of the message she is trying to get across.

Dislikes	Jane has a difficult time controlling her anger, stress, and level of agitation. Her therapist has observed that she lacks the skills necessary to appropriately perceive voice tone, body language, and various communication styles. This fact is often observed by Jane's negative reaction to others attempting to communicate with her. She is prone to inappropriate outburst of anger, yelling, and cursing.

Jane dislikes being told what to do and she states, "I don't like being talked to like a baby." She often is overheard stating "I don't like being ordered around" and "you don't know who you're talking to." Often Jane misperceives other's communication style and makes inappropriate comments as a result.

As stated above, Jane has extreme difficulty in pronouncing words. She gets very agitated when others do not understand what she is attempting to say or when a person pretends to understand what she is saying. Jane will continuously repeat what she is trying to say until the person is able to understand. Often others will walk away out of frustration at the inability to understand her speech. This angers Jane and often leads to displays of agitation and acting out.

Jane is a very structured individual and dislikes it when her routine is disrupted.

At times Jane does not like to be touched. She likes to be the first to initiate touch. |
| **Gifts and Attributes** | Jane is motivated to learn new things and is often much more up to date and informed of matters, current events, and facts than most people giver her credit. Jane is a trivia and movie buff and can speak on a wide range of subjects. Unfortunately, many people do not give her the time to communicate her message or have the ability to understand her speech. When her speech is understood other people are surprised to learn that she has a wonderful sense of humor and grasp on her surroundings.

Jane is very active in her church as well as the ARC, Special Olympics, and Parks and Recreation. She is very driven to try new things and actively participates in various social and recreational outlets. |

Special People in Life and Natural Supports	Jane is very close to her parents, who live in the immediate area, as well as her sisters living out of town. Jane very much looks forward to visits with her family and often speaks proudly of reunions and time spent with relatives. Jane becomes very agitated when her parents are out of town. During this period of time Jane routinely becomes frustrated and acts out in manners such as name calling, yelling, and cursing. Jane has also made friends with several ladies at her residential facility and enjoys their company and companionship.
Life Goals and Dreams	Jane hopes to become as independent as possible in every aspect of her life and states, "I want to do more stuff on my own." Jane is motivated to improve upon life skill areas and states "I don't want people to make fun of me for talking funny." She elaborates on her goals by explaining that she wants to become more proficient in such things as "getting strong and healthy like my Dad," "figuring out more stuff on my own," and "doing things faster." She dreams of "being just like everyone else."
Services Desired	Jane states that she would like to address and improve upon the following areas – Health and Safety Skills Communication Activities of Daily Living Problem Solving Skills Community Access and Utilization

Please List Any Restrictions	Jane's physician has not listed any physical restrictions. However, she is not physically active nor is she physically fit. She eats poorly and is overweight. She does not have a desire to increase physical activity and often chooses to sit opposed to stand, not lift heavy objects, and not walk for long distances. Staff members should be aware of her lack of energy level and opposition to strenuous physical activity.
	In addition, Jane has mild cerebral palsy and is not agile on her feet. She easily loses her balance and requires assistance when getting in and out of vehicles. In addition, she becomes distracted easily making safety a concern when walking, going up/down stairs, and transporting in/out of vehicles.
Other Important Information	Jane is prone to nasal congestion and often complains of headaches and sinus.
	Jane has poor eyesight and should wear her glasses at all times. However, she often loses her glasses or keeps them very dirty (blocking vision).
Endurance	Jane demonstrates consistent attendance for program related activities with the exception of dates missed for minor health related issues (congestion/sinus). Jane does have trouble staying on task, difficulty multi-tasking, and her endurance is low. Jane does not prefer to lift heavy objects, participate in strenuous exercise, or walk for prolonged periods of time.
Fine Motor Skills	Jane has adequate fine motor skills. She can transfer objects from hand to hand and complete tasks requiring the use of her thumb and forefingers. On occasion, she has difficulty with some everyday task such as opening bottles and Tupperware.

Gross Motor Skills	Jane has some difficulties in stepping up and down steps. She moves at a slow and awkward pace. Some physical assistance and support required.
Personal Care & Hygiene	Jane has difficulty (requiring prompting) with personal hygiene care and skills. She is prone to urinary incontinence, yeast infections, and skin rashes. Jane needs to be encouraged to wash her hands and follow a general personal hygiene routine. Jane also requires prompting to follow a bathroom schedule in order to avoid urinary incontinence. In addition, prompting is needed so that she disposes of protective undergarments correctly.
Communication	Jane has difficulty communicating and expressing her thoughts due to speech impairment. However, Jane enjoys communicating and socializing with others. She is angered easily when others do not take the time to understand her speech or pretend to understand what she is saying. Jane does not give up when trying to get a point across and will use sign language, home made signs, gestures, and charade like movements. Jane will pursue her listener until she is sure the person understands and is able to repeat the message back to her. Jane has a large vocabulary and knowledge base to the surprise of many people who do not give her the time or credit. This, understandably, is a major source of stress for Jane.
Socialization	Jane truly loves to be around people, talk to people, and participate in activities with other people. She enjoys being a part of the community and taking part in natural community interactions. However, Jane's socialization skills are limited at times because of her difficulty with speech, mobility, and misinterpretation of other people's voice tones and body language.

Personal Awareness	Jane is very aware of herself, others, and her surroundings. Jane is somewhat aware of personal information such as telephone number and address. However, she requires some prompting and direction for the correct information. Jane is able to state her birth date and describes events from her childhood.
Community Involvement	Jane greatly enjoys community involvement and has a desire for further community participation. Her residential provider and day support provider assist with community involvement. Jane enjoys dinning out at favorite local restaurants in the community.
Money Management	Jane has a very basic concept of money skills. For instance, she knows how much money it cost to purchase a drink from a machine. She is able to recognize pennies, dimes, nickels, and quarters but has trouble with more complex concepts.
Time Management	Jane has a basic understanding of time, reading a clock, and is able to associate the time of day with specific events. However, Jane is frequently late for scheduled events but not as a result of incorrectly telling time. As stated above, she is very ritualistic and will often not begin a new task or attend a scheduled event until she has completed a particular sequence or pattern as she sees fit. Jane often shows little regard to time management and following a set schedule due to the compulsion to complete a ritualistic routine before moving on with her day.

Paul Spicer, QMRP

Behavior	Jane's mood and behavior is highly dependent on how she perceives the intentions of the person or people in which she is socializing. Jane misjudges social cues, voice tone, and body language to the point that it often leads to signs of aggression and verbal abuse. Jane responds very well to people who speak in a fashion that is not perceived as "baby like" or "childlike." Jane is also responsive to a very upbeat, positive, energetic, and humorous approach. Jane wants to see that the person talking to her is taking their time to understand her words and repeating them back to her so that she knows they understand her point. Individuals utilizing these tactics will gain a rapport and sense of trust with Jane. Much of Jane's acting out can be headed off with the correct approach and mindfulness of voice tone and actions.
Safety/Health	Jane has knowledge of basic safety concerns, concepts, and signs. However, she is easily distracted and often does not pay attention. Prompting is required for proper safety procedures.

INDIVIDUALIZED SERVICE PLANS

STEP FOUR: Identifying The Method of Delivery

Only after your client's unique interests, abilities, and vision for the future have been identified – and a functional assessment tool has been utilized – is it possible to begin mapping out a plan to assist the client in reaching their desired goals.

Paul Spicer, QMRP

Knowing your local agency's guidelines and policies are crucial, as this aspect of developing a plan of care becomes much more technical than any other. Most likely a governing body and funding source, such as Medicaid Waiver or CARF, lays the groundwork for how a plan of care can and cannot be created in your locality.

As a healthcare provider or caseworker you will be required to develop a plan of care that is appropriate, client centered, and measurable as determined by your governing body. This plan of care is often referred to as an individualized service plan, consumer service plan, or client service plan. No matter the kind of plan of care or governing source – several common themes hold true in most scenarios. Perhaps the most important is identifying "goals" and "objectives" for your client. All client goals and objectives should be recorded and laid out in such a fashion that demonstrates a clear-cut road map to independence.

I. Goals and Objectives:

Understand The Difference Between Goals Versus Objectives:

GOALS	OBJECTIVES
Goals are long-term	Objectives are short-term
Goals are large in scope and touch upon many life areas	Objectives are more specific and pin-point specific tasks
Goals may or may not be in immediate grasp	Objectives are smaller, more manageable steps leading to a goal
Goals represent a client's dream come true	Objectives represent the everyday tasks and steps necessary to reach that dream
Goals are generally smaller in number – as they are larger covering wide reaching skills	Objectives can be more plentiful as they serve as a method or path to reach the larger goal
Goals may take a longer time to accomplish	Objectives are generally more obtainable in a shorter period of time

Everyone should have goals. What are your client's goals for today? For tomorrow? For next month? For next year?

A carefully designed plan of care will develop a roadmap to help your client reach their goals. Along the way there will be a number of smaller steps or objectives, that will need to be addressed first before reaching the final outcome.

Below you will find examples of goals and objectives. Pay careful attention to how objectives support the end result and pave the path to the client's ultimate goal.

Examples of Goals and Objectives

GOAL: Hunter wishes to make more friends and socialize with others.

OBJECTIVE: Hunter will practice communication skills with staff members and peers on a daily basis in order to make more friends.

GOAL: Kylie would like to obtain employment as a cashier at a fast food restaurant.

OBJECTIVE: Kylie will practice identifying various coin and bill denominations to prepare for a job as a cashier.

GOAL: Ryan would like to better manage his anger.

OBJECTIVE: Ryan will practice stress management techniques on a daily basis in order to control his anger.

GOAL: Corey would like to improve his health and well-being.

OBJECTIVE: Corey will address an exercise routine each day, so that to improve overall health.

ASSISTANCE vs. TRAINING

Once you understand the difference between goals and objectives, it is highly important to differentiate between the many possible ways to implement a plan of care. As a healthcare provider or caseworker you will need to determine the best method to address your client's objectives in order to meet their final goal.

Determining the best course of action relies heavily on your delivery method. Quite simply, the delivery method can be broken down into two formats – a) assistance/maintenance in nature or b) training in nature.

    a. <u>Assistance/Maintenance Objectives:</u> In this capacity, the objective's focus would rest on the client's desire to simply address an ongoing aspect of daily life. The focus would be placed purely on addressing, participating in, and maintaining a skill. Staff members would be required to assist the individual to address this skill in order of maintaining a desired level of functioning. Sometimes referred to as, "maintenance" or "participatory objective."

    b. <u>Training Objectives:</u> On the other hand, a training objective focuses more on improving upon a skill, rather than just maintaining or participating in it. In this scenario the client has chosen a life area that he or she would like to work towards a higher level of functioning. Staff members would be required to train the client on particular techniques to improve functioning and independence level. In this scenario, careful notes and data would be collected to track progress.

In other words.....an assistance objective works to maintain a skill, where as a training objective works to improve upon a desired skill.

Because of the many aspects of any given human being, it is entirely possible to have both assistance and training objectives in a single plan of care. For instance, Chris may have mastered the skill of proper hygiene and healthcare, but still require minor assistance on a daily basis in order to maintain this skill. At the same time, Chris may lack a network of friends and have difficulty communicating, leading to the need for communication training performed by a staff member.

INDIVIDUALIZED SERVICE PLANS

STEP FIVE: Designing Measurable Outcomes

Measurable goals/objectives are like a ladder, it has rungs —which tell you where you are in your climb, and when you've reached the top.

Effectiveness in achieving a program's goals and objectives is established by defining each goal and objective by measurable outcomes. Data relating to each of the outcomes can then be used to ascertain to what extent each goal and objective has been achieved.

When developing a plan of care it is important to keep in mind the desired outcome of the services provided. Outcomes are benefits, or changes, for an individual during or after participating in program activities. Outcomes may relate to behavior, skills, knowledge, attitude, condition, or other attributes. They are what the individuals knows, thinks, can do; or how they behave; or what their condition is, that is different following the program.

Developing a complete and specific plan of care ensures that the services provided will address the identified need. In this fashion, the training you deliver will be pertinent, current, consistent and easily documented. Again, it must be <u>measurable</u> so that accurate documentation can take place.

Below you'll find the five basic steps to complete this process:

INDENTIFY AND SPECIFIY

1) Identify the client's goal that you would like to assist/train so that to make a desired change. Clearly indicate what is the desired change.

2) Identify what the goal will look like once the change has occurred. Define if this means an *increase, a decrease,* or *to maintain.*

3) Specify the amount of change that will signify a successful result. Apply the terms: How Much, *How Often, How Long.*

4) Specify how you will document the change. Decide where you will get data on *How Much, How Often, How Long* – in measurable terms.

5) Specify what condition should result from the successful provision of a service.

So what can I "MEASURE"?

First, ask your client what he or she wants to measure! What are their goals, their desired outcomes, and their vision for the future? Identify possible outcomes by brainstorming knowledge, skills, and behaviors, etc. that your client wants to display when they have finished the program. Review the brainstormed possible outcomes and select those that best reflect those outcomes that are essential to your assessment plan. Next, translate these outcomes into the language of specific, measurable, observable behaviors.

There are NO specific categories for outcomes, nor are there any right or wrong outcomes. Below you will find suggestions for several broad categories that can serve only as a framework in this endeavor. These categories may be helpful as you brainstorm possible outcomes.

Complex cognitive skills- Reflective thought, critical thinking, quantitative reasoning, and intellectual flexibility.

Knowledge acquisition- Subject matter mastery and knowledge application.

Intrapersonal development- Autonomy, identity, aesthetics, self-esteem, and maturity.

Practical competence- Career preparation, managing one's personal affairs, and economic self-sufficiency.

Civic responsibility- Responsibilities as a citizen in a democratic society and commitment to democratic ideals.

Academic achievement- The ability to earn satisfactory grades in courses.

Persistence- The ability to pursue a degree to graduation or achieve personal educational objectives.

In short, revisit the functional assessment that details the client's skills and deficits. This shall provide you with the best picture of appropriate outcomes.

No Fuzzy Objectives

Consider These Fuzzy Objectives:

Bob will increase self-sufficiency.

Bob will reduce violence.

Staff will help Bob feel good about himself.

Why Are These Objectives So Bad:

Where is the specific task, the specific steps, the endpoint, the desired change, the result, and the impact?

What condition should result from the successful provision of a service?

What is the desired time frame?

How will you measure the process, and state how you will know when the service has been successful?

Where are the measurable terms?

How can you specify if he or she has accomplished this objective?

How much of a particular service will the program provide during a given period?

What is specifically going to happen as result of that service provision?

How Could These Objectives Be Improved Upon:

Bad Objective:

Bob will increase self-sufficiency.

Good Objective:

Bob will improve upon self-sufficiency by independently addressing oral hygiene (or any other task that Bob selects, be specific). Bob will address this task three times a day at his residential facility. Staff will provide training techniques to include verbal and physical prompting. Bob will complete this objective when he has independently, without prompting from staff, brushed his teeth on 20 consecutive trials, with 90% accuracy. Target date is June 30, 2005.

Bad Objective:

Bob will reduce violence.

Good Objective:

Bob will improve upon stress management skills by implementing deep breathing techniques opposed to violence when agitated. Bob will address these skills on a daily basis in the home and work environment. Staff will provide training techniques to include verbal prompting, visual cues, and biofeedback. Bob will complete this objective when he demonstrates the ability to independently implement such techniques, without prompting from staff. Bob will complete this objective when he demonstrates the ability to utilize these skills with 100% accuracy on 30 consecutive trials. Target date is March 1, 2005.

How To Set Criteria

Healthcare providers must always set a criterion for each and every objective so that it is clear to the client and trainer when the task at hand has been successfully completed.

In other words, create an end point or a desired outcome which can be measured such that to demonstrate clear mastery of a skill. For example, set a success rate, percentage point, or mastery level such as "Bob will know that he has completed this task when it is addressed correctly on "X" amount of trials."

Healthcare workers need to pay careful attention so that to document the progression of the skill at hand so that to cease or continue training accordingly. If a client clearly demonstrates mastery of a skill, you as the healthcare worker are ethically required to cease billing and training in that area.

However, if mastering a skill leads to the development of a new goal, and thus a new set of criterion, redevelop the client's plan of care accordingly.

Remember, your job is to help guide your client along a roadmap of clearly defined goals and objectives. That roadmap must include realistic checkpoints, or criterion, so that the client knows he or she is progressing in the correct fashion.

INDIVIDUALIZED SERVICE PLANS

STEP SIX: Monitoring The Integrity of Data

Staff members must develop an observant eye and reporter-like ability to record purely the facts. This must be taught, developed, emphasized, and renewed.

Paul Spicer, QMRP

So how can you ensure good data management?

A quality plan of care, no matter how well designed, is of little use should you fail to accurately monitor the progress of your client. The method in which the plan of care you are implementing, and the quality of the care you are providing, must always be recorded in an honest and straightforward fashion.

Internal reviewers, as well as those from outside your agency, should be performed so that to systematically check for quality assurance and to determine that you as an agency are appropriately billing funding sources (such as Medicaid) for services that you are in fact providing.

The information you collect on actual goals and objectives is known as "data," and should always reflect the progress of the client truthfully, if not, the client and the agency as a whole will suffer. Many licenses have been lost, facilities shut down, and clients treated poorly due to poor data management.

So how can you ensure good data management?

It must be a general philosophy adopted from each and every manager and administrator down to all direct staff members carrying out the plan of care. A skilled service provider, and agency as a whole, must sense when a client is confused – and document it; when a client is becoming disinterested – and document it; when a client is scared – and document it; when a client is confident – and document it; when a client is exhausted - and document it; and when a client is up for a new challenge – and document it.

In short, a service agency must step into the client's shoes and feel what they are feeling. Simply put, staff members must develop an observant eye and reporter-like ability to record purely the facts. This must be taught, developed, emphasized, and renewed.

Here's how:

Rule of Thumb:

IF YOU DIDN"T RECORD IT, IT DIDN"T HAPPEN.

Healthcare providers must always record the training and assistance given to a client, as well as the outcome. If this training is not recorded and the facility fails to keep a record of all data collected, then there is no evidence that the training ever occurred.

IF IT DIDN"T HAPPEN, YOU CANNOT GET PAID

If there is no evidence that training has occurred, nor any record of client progress, you cannot expect as a facility to be reimbursed for services rendered. You must show that you are carrying out the plan of care as agreed upon by you and the client.

DOCUMENT, DOCUMENT, DOCUMENT

Let no detail go unnoticed, the more the better. A detailed account of all services is the only way to ensure that you are meeting the needs of your client and fulfilling your obligations as a service provider.

YOUR ROLE

- Always keep accurate documentation. Record what you observed in an objectionable fashion, with no personal feelings or ulterior motives.

- Record what you see, hear, and observe – everything factual.

- Never "fudge" documentation – no matter what.

- If you don't understand how a goal or objective is to be documented, then ask.

- Ensure that the data collected reflects the services as outlined in the plan of care.

- Remember that all data collected is subject for review by supervisors, administrators, quality control teams, as well as outside licensing and funding agencies.

- Realize that everything and anything you record could at some point be subpoenaed for legal action or appeal hearing.

Tell-Tale Signs of Poor Data Collection

Each and every service provider is required to maintain some sort of documentation that proves that services are being delivered as spelled out in the client's plan of care. Formats and styles of documentation may vary from agency to agency, yet all are required to document their work.

Many agencies arrange for internal teams to review the data collected and/or require staff to routinely monitor their own data collection methods so that to catch mistakes before it's too late. In any event, all data is subject for review by funding, licensing, and governmental agencies – many of which have the ability to shut a program down for poor data collection and/or require a reimbursement of funds, sometimes totaling millions of dollars.

Here's what reviewers are looking for when auditing data collection:

The use of whiteout or eraser ink -- Not only does it look bad, it is often not allowed by training facilities and governing agencies.

Blue, red, or purple ink -- Again, multi-colored ink looks bad and is generally not allowed. Black ink is always a much better choice.

Blacked-out or scribbled through data – If you make an error, never try to hide it. Simply, mark through errors with a single line, sign/initial, and date any changes to the record.

Opinions and hunches -- Should never be used. If absolutely necessary to include an opinion, make sure you clearly state that it is just that – your opinion.

Unsigned data -- Perhaps the biggest red flag, unsigned data is most often sited by utilization review staff. Any time data is recorded it must be accompanied by a signature or initials of the specific staff that provided the service. If no signature is provided, the data is worthless.

Undated data -- Similarly, all data should be dated.

Lacking Full Name – Documents should never be filled out using a client's nickname or first name. Full names should be utilized at all times.

Completed Objectives— That is to say, any sign that the client has progressed to the point that a desirable level of independence has been reached and the objective is no longer necessary. If the goal has been reached, you can no longer bill for it.

Useless Objectives -- Any objective that continues to be refused, or turned down, by a client may need to be revaluated for its appropriateness.

UNDERSTAND WHY YOU ARE COLLECTING DATA

Data should not be collected just for the sake of collecting it. Nor should it be collected only because an outside governing body requires you to do so. Instead, data collection is a tool utilized by healthcare professionals to ensure all services rendered accurately reflect the plan agreed upon by all parities.

The end result of the data should be to determine if the services are helpful and beneficial, or if they are not working and changes need to be made. Therefore, data should be routinely monitored for four things:

---

1) Improvements In Skill Level

2) Maintenance of Skill Level

3) Decrease In Skill Level

4) Refusal To Participate

In each scenario, the data collected tells the service provider how successful is the plan of care. If the data collected demonstrates that a client is routinely mastering a skill, improvement has been made, or a criteria level has been reached – then it is necessary to reassess the appropriateness of a specific goal or objective.

For example, if Joe sets a goal to independently wash his clothes on twenty consecutive trials, and he has now mastered that skill, it is now time to determine if the goal should be discontinued or adjusted to better meet his new needs. Perhaps now Joe may want to address not only washing his clothes but drying them too. If a client is fully independent, and the objective is no longer relevant, then funding sources, licensing agents, and reviewers will want to know why data is continuing to be tracked and why money is continuing to be spent on an objective that has been completed.

Similarly, if an objective continues to be refused or turned down by a client it should send up red flags to staff members that the objective needs to be revaluated. If the data collected reflects that a client routinely opts not to participate in the objective, it should be discontinued and changed to meet the client's new needs.

For this reason we see why accurate data must be collected at all times. Once it is collected, however, the data must continue to be reviewed and assessed so that to take appropriate action. Above all the data should be accurate, and not sloppily compiled or falsely reported. Never comprise the integrity of the data.

INDIVIDUALIZED SERVICE PLANS

STEP SEVEN: Recording Notes And Observations

All notes and observations should support the individualized plan of care, and demonstrate how that plan is being carried out.

Key Indicators

Often called progress notes or ID Notes, the written observations recorded are key indicators of how a client is progressing towards their goals and vision for the future. Like the data collected on a client, the notes and observations collected are also required by governing bodies and thus fall under strict scrutiny.

Rightfully so, the notes and observations collected can be subpoenaed or court ordered, and often serve as documentation that proves a service provider did or did not deliver services to a client. For this reason, along with the fact that good documentation improves good services, it is highly important for staff members to develop their writing and note taking skills.

All notes and observations should support the individualized plan of care, and demonstrate how that plan is being carried out. By doing so, progress and ID Notes should mirror and support the data being collected for the plan of care. For instance, if data demonstrates that Joe is excelling at all goals related to community living, the ID notes should also reflect Joe's improving skill level.

Progress notes have the ability to go even further than simple data collection. These notes provide an extended format for you to lay out your client's current situation. A good note taker has the ability to record significant events, no mater how small, and relay those events to the person's over all plan of care.

Good Note vs Bad Note

Bad Note – Mary Lou had a bad week at her day support program.

Good Note – Mary Lou arrived at the day support program today and was observed to be agitated, as evidenced by flushed face, verbal outbursts, and frustration expressed to staff members. Staff encouraged Mary Lou to take a little time to herself in the stress management room, where she listened to calming music and practiced relaxation techniques. Afterwards Mary Lou and staff discussed her level of frustration, which she explained as, "I'm just so darn sick of my bus driver, I don't know what to do." Staff provided Mary Lou with a number of stress management techniques through a series of role play, and at Mary Lou's request have arranged for a team meeting to include her bus driver and a circle of supports Mary Lou has asked to be present.

ELEMENTS OF GOOD NOTES AND OBSERVATIONS

- A good note should include the onset and duration of physical, mental, or behavioral symptoms.

- A good note provides facts, not opinions.

- A good note is straightforward and reports what is observed without including exaggerated expressions, slang, or preconceived notions.

- A good note may refer to relevant developmental history and previous interventions and outcomes if it applies to the current situation.

- A good note includes current medical and mental health conditions or symptoms.

- A good note reflects any fluctuations in weight, eating, bathroom, or sleeping habits.

- A good note may include current medications, including types, reasons taking, side effects, medication history, current supports, skills, or problems administering.

- A good note reports any allergies and special diets, if any, and why.

- A good note reports any special limitations to activities and why.

- A good note discusses the client's abilities and difficulties in adapting to a goal, to change, to personal disappointment, or to frustrating experiences.

- A good note relays comments, thoughts, and quotes by the client.

- A good note follows up on concerns. For example, if you indicated that a client is having difficulty managing daily living skills, you should indicate what you as a staff member are doing to remedy the situation.

- A good note has a clear interest and concern over the client's health and well being. If you indicated a health concern in the note, make sure to indicate and follow up on what you are doing about the concern.

- A good note demonstrates the client's personal preferences and desires – things that make he or she feel good and successful, as well as things that make the person feel bad or unsuccessful.

- A good note reports resources, services, and supports needed to assist and/or train the client.

GOOD PROGRESS NOTE/BAD PROGRESS NOTE? You Decide!

EXAMPLE ONE:

7/04 Ricky had a good night. – W. Smith.

Good or Bad? Why?

Hint: Is the date accurately reported? Did the staff member fill out their entire name and title? Did the person writing the note capture the essence of the client and the issue at hand in a detailed and factual manner?

EXAMPLE TWO:

07/14/04: Frances got out of bed four times tonight, attempting to take clothing items from her housemates. Staff redirected her back to the bed each time and she fell asleep soundly from 3 am to 7 am. – William Sanders, Residential Training Specialist

Good or Bad? Why?

EXAMPLE THREE:

June: This was a bad month for James. I think he was in a bad mood because he was mean to me. – Chris Taylor

Good or Bad? Why?

Hint: Is the date accurately reported? Does the date contain the specific month, day, and year? Did the staff member fill out their entire name and title? Did the person writing the note use gross generalizations and personal feelings?

EXAMPLE FOUR:

10/23/04: Jim did not corporate with staff on this date. He refused to change his soiled clothing, and would not shower. Staff members stressed the importance of proper hygiene and physically modeled appropriate care of soiled clothing as well as demonstrated cleaning techniques. Jim reported to staff that he was frustrated due to not getting a break at his job earlier today. He indicated that he was angry, wanted to quit, and not go in tomorrow morning. Morning staff should be aware of Jim's state of mind and attempt to encourage Jim to wash clothing if he decides to go to work. Jim's case manager and job coach were called this evening and will meet Jim in the morning to discuss his employment options.

- TS

Good or Bad? Why?

Hint: Even if the note itself is excellent, did the staff member fill out his or her name and title in the correct fashion?

EXAMPLE FIVE:

12/04: Todd was really good today; I think he likes me working with him. I like the red shirt he was wearing today. – Rodney Harrison, Assistant Day Support Staff

Good or Bad? Why?

Hint: Is the date accurately reported? Does the date contain the specific month, day, and year? Did the person writing the note report on factual information and observations, or merely use personal feelings?

Progress Notes Should Reflect the Unique Needs of the Client

Make every attempt to reflect the unique character of the client in all progress notes. In this way you keep at the forefront of your mind the need for all services to be directed by the client and for the betterment of his or her well being.

Below you'll find examples of exerts from progress notes that take into account the client, and what it is that he or she hopes to receive from their plan of care:

Good – Client Centered – Observation:

Emily expressed today that she wants to take better care of her teeth. She says that she'd like to have someone to help her with this, but not tell her what she has to do all the time.

Good – Client Centered – Observation:

Billy wants someone to be there at his apartment when he gets home from dialysis, as he reports feeling tired and poorly upon his return.

Good – Client Centered – Observation:

Greg was quoted as saying today, "I'm just tired of staff telling me what to do all the time, especially when I already know how to do it."

Good – Client Centered – Observation:

Brittany stated on this date that she wanted to be more independent and make her own decisions. Brittany states, "I want to be Miss Independent!"

INDIVIDUALIZED SERVICE PLANS

STEP EIGHT: Writing Quarterly Reports

The quarterly report serves as a compilation and summary of all the observations noted in progress notes, data collected on skill level, and statements made by the client over a three-month period of time. This report should always be written in a factual manner that is driven by the client's needs, wants, and desires.

Paul Spicer, QMRP

Why Write a Quarterly Report?

In almost all localities anyone providing Medicaid-reimbursed or CARF-sactioned residential support, personal assistance, day support, and pre-vocation services must complete quarterly reports documenting the effectiveness of services rendered.

The quarterly report, completed in a timely manner once every three months, serves as the perfect companion to the client's plan of care or individualized service plan (ISP). In this manner, the quarterly report becomes an extension of the original plan of care, and should complement the goals and objectives laid out in that plan.

A well-written quarterly report documents the strategies utilized by the training staff and how these strategies are affecting the client's ability to achieve the goals and objectives as outlined in the plan of care/ISP. The quarterly report is not only a good idea, but is often required by licensing and governing bodies in order to show that services are delivered as outlined in the ISP.

In effect, the quarterly report serves as a compilation and summary of all the observations noted in progress notes, data collected on skill level, and statements made by the client over a three month period of time. This report should always be written in a factual manner that is driven by the client's needs, wants, and desires.

That is to say, the quarterly report should always be person-centered in nature and document the client's ability to address the aspects of life that he or she has identified as most important. A well-written quarterly report demonstrates the client's strengths, interests, and support needs over a set period of time. The report should be functional, and all information should be gathered through a variety of means in order to determine the client's current abilities to participate in daily affairs.

In short, the quarterly report provides a snap shot in time, a document of the client's current status and ability to address the world in which he or she lives. After reading a well-written quarterly report you should be able to clearly identify an individual's strengths and interests, and most importantly – how to best build upon them.

The following is a description of each of the components necessary in writing a quality quarterly report that meets all documentation requirements.

COMPONENTS OF A QUARTERLY REPORT

Every agency should develop their own method of documenting quarterly progress. No two agencies will have the same method, just as no two clients will have the same information shared on the quarterly report. You must find out what makes the most sense for your agency, and most important for your client.

However, there is a common vein running through well-written quarterly reports – and that is person centered reporting. All documents should demonstrate that the client's own personal vision is being addressed on a daily basis. To demonstrate this, a good quarterly report will include at least some of the following components.

Current Status – Demonstrate the client's current state of being. What is the individual's current state of mind? How is their mood and character? How is their home life? How is their financial situation? How are their transportation and other resources?

Type and Need of Service – Demonstrate the need for continuation of services, or discontinuation of services as related to what was reported in the "Current Status" section. For example, if you report that currently your client is experiencing "Situational Anger Disorder," you should follow up with documentation related to what type of services are needed at this time and what you as an agency are doing to address this need. A well-written quarterly report justifies why a service is needed at this time, or why it is being discontinued.

Critical Incidents - Record all incidents, negative and positive, that demonstrates a substantial impact on the client's physical or mental health, safety, and well being. Include dates, observations, and outcomes.

Health Status – Document the health status of the client and reflect the degree to which a person is able to function physically, emotionally, and socially, with or without aid from a particular agency. Remember, if an aspect of a person's health status is comprised, remember to document what it is that you as a staff member are doing to remedy the situation.

Level of Satisfaction – Document the client's feelings about the effectiveness and appropriateness of the services that he or she receives. To accurately measure client satisfaction you must first determine what is meant by "satisfied." What aspects of daily life are important to the client, and are you honoring these aspects and ensuring these desires are being meet.

Progress - Document the level of improvement, decline, or ability to maintain skills related to the goals and objectives the client has identified as most crucial in their plan of care. Record prompt levels, assistance required, and training tools necessary to address these goals and objective.

Paul Spicer, QMRP

What are "Critical Incidents" and Which of Them Should You Include in a Quarterly Report?

CRITICAL INCIDENTS DEFINED

A "critical incident" is any actual or alleged event or situation that creates a significant change – either positive or negative – in a client's life and plan of care.

Examples of "critical incidents" include:

- Any abuse or neglect of the participant inflicted by others.

- Any misappropriation of the person's funds or property.

- A violation of the person's basic human rights.

- All unexpected, untimely and urgent emergency hospital admissions including any that are or may be the result of substandard care.

- Errors in medical or medication management that result or could result in significant adverse medical reactions or behavioral responses indicating a threat to the person's health.

- The initiation of an investigation by law enforcement authorities of an event or allegation that involves a client either as a perpetrator or victim that may lead to criminal charges.

- All suspected or confirmed suicide attempts by a client.

- A fire in the home or facility in which the client lives or where the participant was receiving services if the fire required the response of a fire department and created a significant risk to the client's health or safety.

- Significant damage to property including but not limited to the property of the client, service providers, to the client's residence, place of employment or other place the participant frequents if such property damage poses or posed a threat to the person's health, safety or welfare.

- Unsafe or unsanitary environmental conditions in a person's home or place where the individual receives services.

- Use of isolation, seclusion, or restraint (physical or chemical) by a service provider.

- Unanticipated absence of the participant including any unauthorized leaving by the participant such as wandering or intentionally leaving which suggest that the participant is at risk of harm.

*Staff should take special note that reporting critical incidents in the quarterly report does not eliminate any other reporting requirements. All other required reporting procedures, such as abuse or caregiver reporting violations of basic human rights, should be completed as to give support to any reporting of critical incidents.

If a Change is Needed....This is the Time!

Consider This Scenario

A client with mental retardation has received assistance from staff over the past six-months on learning to tie his shoes. This client has an objective written into his plan of care relating to the need for assistance while dressing and tying shoes. However, the client recently made the choice to purchase Velcro shoes so that to manage dressing in a more independent fashion without help from staff.

Therefore, the objective is no longer needed and should not remain in the client's plan of care if he or she feels it should cease.

The quarterly report is an ideal time to document this change in services and record why the client no longer desires assistance with dressing and tying his shoes. Remember, the quarterly report provides a snapshot of the progress made over a three-month period of time and therefore justifies why or why not various aspects of the plan of care should be continued or discontinued.

Consider This Scenario

Three months ago a client identified the desire to improve her ability to recognize various coin denominations so that to independently purchase sodas at the drink machine. The client designed training strategies with staff members and set as a criterion ten consecutive trials implemented independently and correctly as the benchmark for success.

Shortly before the end of the quarter, this client mastered the skill and performed the task independently for the number of trials agreed upon. After careful examination, both the client and staff members agreed that she now has the ability to address this task independently.

The quarterly report is an ideal time to document this success, and record the fact that the client has reached the criteria level for the specific task. The quarterly report should show the current level of functioning and justify why the task is no longer going to be addressed in the future. Staff should also include any new objectives or changes at this time. For instance, the quarterly would be an appropriate time to change the objective to now state that the client has mastered the skill of purchasing sodas from a drink machine and would now like to learn to purchase items at a restaurant. A new set of training techniques and criteria level should be developed and recorded in the quarterly report.

Paul Spicer, QMRP

DEMONSTRATE CLINET INVOVLEMENT

Above all else, make sure that the involvement of your client in his or her plan of care is clearly demonstrated. Here's how:

Use quotes – When asked about his plan of care, John states, "yeah, it's pretty cool, at least when ya'll aren't babying me too much." Allow the client's real personality to shine through and don't be afraid to include quotes in the quarterly report. If the client is not happy with services, don't be afraid to say so. Make sure to record how the client feels and why the client is or isn't satisfied with services.

Review All Documents and Notes With Clients – Record the interactions that occur between you and your client as related to the review of his or her service plan. For example, state in the quarterly report that you have read and explained to your client all of the notes and data kept that pertains to the client. Explain in your report how you reviewed these materials with your client and what he or she had to say about them. Document their approval or disapproval of what has been recorded.

Have Clients Signed All Quarterly Reports - Demonstrate that you have involved your client in the collection of all data and notes by asking he or she to sign the quarterly report. However, before the client signs the report, you should always read aloud the document in its entirety and make sure that the client understands the meaning of all words. At times, clients with limited reading and writing ability may need pictures or assitive technology to understand what is being reported. Like wise, a check or "X" mark may be required stating that he or she agrees with what has been reported. Have a witness present to ensure that the person interprets the document does so appropriately.

Demonstrate A Collaborative Approach – Make sure to involve all members of a person's circle of supports, as defined by that person. If a client chooses to involve his or her family member, neighbor, or co-worker in his or her care – then respect this choice. Document the involvement of all significant players, and demonstrate how they affect the plan of care. Make sure to record the contact, and collaboration with case managers, residential staff, day support staff, and family members (when appropriate). Make sure to obtain the proper written permission to share or disclose any client information with third parties.

INDIVIDUALIZED SERVICE PLANS

STEP NINE: Reviewing Your Documents

Your agency should place a high priority on quality review and quality control efforts so that to improve client files and documents on an ongoing basis. In doing so you'll determine the overall effectiveness of your plan of care and services as a whole. Gathering co-workers together each week, each month, or at the very least each quarter to review documents is highly recommended no matter the size of the agency or caseload.

Paul Spicer, QMRP

THE REVIEW PROCESS SHOULD PRODUCE CLEAR ANSWERS TO THE FOLLOWING QUESTIONS:

How will the client's life be changed as a result of your services, i.e., will the client have increased competence; will the client's status be improved; will the client have opportunities for more people in their life; will the client have opportunities to do things they enjoy as well as new and stimulating things, etc?

Is the plan of care and services rendered made up of effective staff that can train/assist the client, while supplementing one another's talents?

Is the plan of care, and the agency as a whole, capable of carrying out all necessary responsibilities to act in the best interest of the client?

Are roles and responsibilities clearly defined in the plan of care, and are they clearly understood by both client and staff members?

Is there an effective working relationship between client, staff, and agency?

Does the client, as well as staff members implementing the plan, fully understand the mission of the plan of care and how that mission is achieved through their actions?

Do the staff members of the agency, with the guidance of the client, collectively formulate specific goals to guide the plan?

Does the agency seek and use client input <u>at all times</u> during the planning process?

Are the client's goals and objectives clearly stated and written in a way that anyone could understand the purpose of the plan of care?

What assurance is there that the interest of the client is well represented?

Is the client benefiting from the plan of care?

Is their a connection and collaboration between the client, the staff members, and the agency?

Do the supports offered teach the client to use the community and community resources with and without agency staff?

File Review Check Off List.

• **Drug Use Profile/ Emergency Medical Information**	Is there clear information present that describes the client's current medical situation, allergies, medications, and conditions? *YES* *NO*

Does the "Drug Use Profile" and "Emergency Information" reflect current medications and appropriate administration? *YES* *NO*

Has it been updated in the last year? YES *NO*

Are physicians/hospital preferences current? YES NO

Have all recent significant medical problems been noted? YES NO |
| • **Application** | Is there an application present which shows the start and need for services? *YES* *NO* |
| • **Orientation** | Is there documentation of an orientation/explanation of services, and clear example of the client's knowledge of the services they are receiving? *YES* *NO*

Are all areas of training documented, signed, dated?

YES *NO* |
| • **Physical Exam** | Is there a copy of the client's physical exam present? *YES* *NO*

Was the physical exam performed within 30-days of admission to services and proper documentation kept?

YES *NO* |
| • **Legal Rights** | Is there clear evidence and documentation that the client's human rights have been explained?

YES NO

Have the human rights been reviewed and signed by the client (as well as reviewer/witness signatures) and documented at least once a year. YES NO |

• **Releases**	Is there clear evidence and documentation that the client has consented to exchange and/or disclose personal information? *YES NO*

Is there documentation that you as a staff member or agency is allowed to share that information with any other parties? *YES   NO*

Have all consent to exchange or disclose information forms been signed and updated for the current year? *YES   NO*

Does the consent to exchange information form include all appropriate agencies in which the client allows information to be released? *YES   NO*

Is there documentation that the client has consented to attend programming and/or receive services, i.e. "Programming Release." *YES   NO*

Has a "Programming Release" form been signed and updated each year? *YES   NO*

Is there documentation of an "Emergency Care Release" form, or permission for the agency to treat a client in case of emergency? *YES   NO*

Has the "Emergency Care Release" form been signed and updated each year? *YES   NO*

Is there documentation that the client has given permission to have his or her photo taken or name used in any form of media, i.e. "Photo Release"?

YES   NO

Has the "Photo Release" form been signed and updated each year? *YES   NO*

Is there documentation that the client gives permission for the agency to administer or assist in the self-administering of medication, i.e. "Medication Permission" form? *YES   NO*

Has the "Medication Permission" form been signed and updated each year? *YES   NO* |

• **Service Plans**	Is there evidence and documentation of not only your agency's specific service plan, but the entire range of the service system? Is there evidence of collaboration between case management, residential, day support, and vocational services? Do you have documentation of the service plans being addressed by other programs that are also assisting the client? Have you clearly documented the entire range of services offered to the client? *YES NO*
• **Person Centered Planning/Choices**	Is there documentation that the client's personal interests and choices have been taken into consideration in the development of all services, i.e. a "Person Center/Choice" form? YES NO Has the "Person Center/Choice" form been updated each year to clearly reflect the client's likes and dislikes? *YES NO* Have the areas identified in the "Person Centered/Choice" form been reflected and addressed in the client's plan of care? For instance, if the client has stated on this form that he or she hates to dance... then the plan of care should not have an objective that relates to exercise in the form of dance. YES NO
• **Functional Assessment**	Is there documentation of the client's functioning ability, i.e. a functional assessment, diagnostic study, or functioning report? *YES NO* Does the functional assessment show clear deficits and strengths, and are these deficits and strengths appropriately acknowledged in the overall plan or care? *YES NO*
• **Psychological**	Is there a copy of a psychological evaluation present? *YES NO* Does it reflect that the client is cognitively impaired and in need of mental retardation services? *YES NO*

• **Annuals**	Is there documentation of an annual review and report for the current year present? *YES NO* Does the annual report detail the correct hours, units, and services provided? *YES NO* Is the client's full name, Medicaid number, and social security number present? *YES NO* Is there a correct start date and end date to the services? For example, if the plan starts on Oct. 1, 2005 then it will end on Sept. 30, 2006. *YES NO* Is there clear evidence of the client's current status, the type of services required, and the client's goals for the future? *YES NO* Do the documents clearly show a profile of the client, the client's abilities, and the client's deficits? *YES NO* Do the client's goals tie into the needs pointed out in the assessment of the client's current status and need for services at this time? *YES NO* For example, if the client's current status says that he or she has difficulty communicating with peers, then it would make sense to have a goal that relates to communication. *YES NO* Do all goals and objectives have target dates that clearly show a timeframe of when the task is to be completed? *YES NO* Does each objective clearly represent a "training" or "assistance" objective? *YES NO*

Does each "training" objective have a clear criterion? For example, "This objective will be considered complete when Joe independently performs this task, without prompting, on twenty consecutive trials." *YES NO*

Does each objective clearly state how often it will be performed/addressed? For example, "Joe will independently apply toothpaste to brush bristles twice a day." *YES NO*

Are all potential barriers to services identified and complete with staff interventions in place? For example, Joe may have a barrier of services that relates to his difficulty with addressing his oral hygiene objective. If so, there needs to be a staff intervention, training technique, or assistance method in place so that Joe may be able to overcome this b*arrier to service. YES NO*

Do the training objectives cover too many steps? *YES NO*

NOTE: For instance, a safety objective should not be too broad by stating, "Joe will improve his independence on safety skills by looking both ways before crossing the street, walking at an appropriate pace while in the building, and maintaining appropriate personal space with others."

This kind of wording would make it impossible to measure one particular skill. What if he was independent in crossing the street and walking at an appropriate speed, but not independent in maintaining appropriate space with others? In this scenario there would be no way to collect data to reflect independence levels in all areas.

It would be more appropriate to say, "Joe will improve safety skills by independently remembering to look both ways before crossing the street." Then the writer could develop another objective that relates to another specific safety areas such as "walking at an appropriate speed while in the building."

Are all training objectives measurable? *YES   NO*

Is it clear what is being measured? *YES   NO*

NOTE: Are you measuring the client's ability to remember to perform the task? Or are you measuring the client's ability to perform a specific step in the task? For example, if it is stated that Joe will independently brush his teeth then it should be clear what is expected and what is being measured. Will he brush his teeth after a staff member puts the toothpaste on the bristles? The objective needs to be specific so that data is collected correctly and client's success is measured appropriately.

It is important to note that at the same time it is also good not to be overly specific such that a writer corners his or herself, as well as their client, into one area. For example, if the objective is written, "Joe will buy a hotdog from the hotdog stand on 45th Street once a week," then it leaves little room for other community exploration. Joe and the staff member will need to collect data on the stated specific areas. However, if Joe would like to buy this hotdog, the writer could word the objective to states that "Joe will make a purchase of his choice, in the community, once a week."

Is person centered language used throughout the annual?

For example, "Joe would like to improve his communication skills" opposed to "Joe will improve his communication skills." Even better, use the client's direct quotes for what he or she would like to do.

YES   NO

Is there a signature page, which is fully filled out by all appropriate parities, that clearly details involvement in the service plan? At the minimum there should be signatures for the client and the person providing the plan.

YES   NO

	Is there a master activity sheet or schedule that details where and when each objective will be addressed?
	YES NO

Quarterlies:	Is there documentation of a quarterly review of the service plan that reports on the client's progress?
	YES NO
	Note: A quarterly report is an extension to the individualized service plan and thus should reflect the following information:
	Are health issues clearly stated in the quarterly? If a health issue is brought up then it should be clearly documented as to what steps were taken to address this issue. For example, "Joe fell while walking to the van on January 1, 2004 and sprained his ankle." In such a case, there should be documented steps such as, "Staff asked Joe not to move while they examined him for physical harm. Joe reported that his ankle hurt and that he would like to be seen by a doctor. Staff transported Joe to the doctor of his choice. Staff reported the incident to the transportation provider, called the residential provider, and filled out an accident report. The next day Joe returned to the program with his doctor's written permission."
	The same thing would apply to behavioral issues. For example, if it was written that, "Staff observed Joe talking with himself and reporting to hear voices" then all steps taken to remedy this situation should be documented.
	Is person centered language utilized in each quarterly? For example, "Joe states that he is very satisfied with his current service plan and feels that it is very beneficial to his overall goal of increased independence." *YES NO*
	Does each quarterly address the client's satisfaction with services and make a case for or against continued service? *YES NO*
	Does each quarterly take into account the client's progress, level of functioning and satisfaction when making changes to the plan? *YES NO*

	Does each quarterly show that collaboration has been made with appropriate parities? For example, the case manager, residential provider, family, etc were active in the plan. *YES NO*
	Does each quarterly take into account and comment on the client's involvement in reviewing their progress and making suggestions. Ex: "Joe and staff carefully reviewed his progress on all objectives. Joe understands each objective and feels that the data collected appropriately reflects his performance." *YES NO*
• **Data & Notes**	Is all data for the current year being kept up to date? *YES NO*
	Is the data filed accompanied by progress notes/ID notes that review the month's significant events? *YES NO*
	Do the progress and ID notes demonstrate the client's current status? *YES NO*
	Do the notes reflect health issues? *YES NO*
	Do the notes demonstrate the client's satisfaction level? *YES NO*
	Are all entries signed with staff name and title? *YES NO*
	Has any whiteout been used? *YES NO*
	Has black ink been used? *YES NO*
	Are there any large gaps between ID note entries? *YES NO*
	Are there any unexplained prolonged absences? *YES NO*
	Does the ID note content reflect the data collected? *YES NO*
	Has each objective been addressed and data recorded? *YES NO*

Are there any gaps in data collected? *YES NO*

Has each objective been addressed exactly as it is stated in the service plan? *YES NO*

Has the criteria been met on any objectives? For example, the criteria of the objective may state that the client has met the objective once he or she has independently addressed the area on twenty consecutive trials. The objective should be discontinued, changed, or updated if the data shows that the client has in fact met the criteria he or she has set for themselves. This is very important for billing issues. *YES NO*

Have staff noted all absences, barriers to services, or "chose not to participate" status appropriately?

YES NO

Are the data sheets signed by every staff member that has recorded data? *YES NO*

Does the data correspond with ID notes? For example, if data shows that on a particular day an abnormal number of prompts were utilized then the ID notes should not state that the person was independent for the day.

YES NO

Has an effort been made to demonstrate any changes in the delivery of service? For example, have staff documented an event when the objective's scheduling was altered or an objective was not addressed?

YES NO

INDIVIDUALIZED SERVICE PLANS

STEP TEN: Implementing The Plan

The ability to observe the client's learning progress and provide new information in just the right amount and at just the right time is the essence of good teaching and can lead to better care.

Paul Spicer, QMRP

Full Potential

Moving into a new era marked with, slow but steady, improvement for individuals with disabilities we must find new ways to integrate individuals of all ability levels into every day life. This includes medical care, exercise opportunities, activities of leisure, and recreational pursuits in order to develop social and physical growth.

In our effort to improve these services, a well written individualized service plan is crucial. In this endeavor, it is important to remember that every client is different, and thus no two plans should be the same. For instance, an individual with Down Syndrome is more at risk for atlantoaxial instability and gait disturbance, possibly requiring physical assistance that should be documented in the individual's plan of care.

Similarly, persons with cerebral palsy, brain injury, spinal cord injury, and stroke may all face spasticity in areas such as the quadriceps muscles, leading to joint pain and requiring physical accommodations or possibly home visits to residential facilities or nursing homes – all of which should be documented.

Like wise, a person with a spinal cord injury may be at risk for thermoregulatory dysfunction because of the reduced capacity to sweat. At the same time, if there is a high-level spinal cord injury, this person must not exceed a heartbeat rate of 90-beat per minute. Again, it is crucial to reflect these unique situations in the plan of care, and keep them in mind when carrying out this plan.

In each of these cases it becomes obvious why extensive information is needed to identify health and social issues that might affect a person's overall plan and how it is to be implemented. Involving case managers, therapists, rehab specialists, and family members can be helpful in determining the best implementation.

Often called 'soft' or 'people' skills, the manner in which the plan of care is implemented is of paramount importance. The ability to observe the client's learning progress and provide new information in just the right amount and at just the right time is the essence of good teaching and can lead to better care.

Here's how….

Quick Tips

- Prompt your clients to keep working on skills of independence, even if it is challenging and the person may not succeed. People with disabilities should not be pitied and handed wins/false accomplishments, just because they have a disability.

- Record the positive successes of your clients, not just the negative ones. Document the effort involved in obtaining the goal at hand and learn from what strategies worked best.

- Observe a person's body actions (eyes, face, arms/hands, posture/stance, etc.) while working with your client. Some clients with disabilities may not readily express discomfort.

- Initiate eye contact and introduce yourself to your client, just as you would with any new acquaintance.

- Acknowledge the presence of a client with a disability even if he or she is unable to communicate.

- Smile in response to communicative attempts and observe the body language of your client.

- It is appropriate to shake hands with a client who has a disability, even if they have limited use of their hands or wear an artificial limb.

- Remember that a person with a disability is not "handicapped," but a "person with a disability." Emphasize the person first.

- Respect personal space and understand that a person's wheelchair is an extension of their body.

- It is OK to use expressions like "running along" when speaking to a wheelchair user or "good to see you" when speaking to a person who is blind. It is likely that they will use similar expressions.

- When a wheelchair user transfers out of the wheelchair to a toilet, car or bed, do not move the wheelchair out of reaching distance.

Paul Spicer, QMRP

Quick Tips

- Concentrate on concrete ideas and skills, while avoiding abstract concepts if the person has a developmental disability.

- Make teaching instructions clear and concise when training a client. Break directions down into small steps or more manageable tasks when needed.

- Demonstrate whenever possible. Showing is often more effective than telling.

- Individuals with hyper activity disorder or mental retardation may have difficulty screening out extraneous stimuli. Cease activity to attend to communication, eliminate outside noise, bright lights, and/or visual distractions.

- Despite the positive progression in the acceptance of individuals with disabilities, those with varying degrees of physical and cognitive deficits are still at times treated like second-class citizens when it comes to participation in community life. Remember this, and remember that you are helping shape the attitudes others have in regard to persons with disabilities.

- Be a role model, people in the community will often look to you to see how best to interact with a person with a disability. Make show you show respect in your actions, body language, and communication style. Pass it along to others.

- Encourage your clients, many who whom have never experienced inclusive opportunities and age-appropriate activities, to fully participate along side non-disabled peers in taking charge of their lives.

- Don't be afraid to offer new suggestions, assistance, and training routines.

- Present healthy opportunities with enthusiasm, energy, and a positive outlook on what the person can achieve with the right accommodations and support.

- Do not react with pity, anxiety, or a variety of other negative emotions when a person is not able to complete a task or goal.

- Prompting and encouraging should not be delivered in a condescending or child-like manner, but instead with sincere enthusiasm for the unique skills and characteristics the person possesses.

- Encourage participation in decision-making roles such as voter, jury duty, board member, etc.

- Encourage participation in community activities i.e., ballet, opera, theatre, sporting events, bingo, movies, cultural activities, etc.

- Promote the ownership of personal belongings and possessions i.e., television, VCR, CD player, furniture, etc.

- Demonstrate and encourage attire that is fashionable, attractive, and age appropriate.

- Model and encourage appropriate friendships and reciprocal relationships i.e. being a good neighbor, volunteering, being a good brother, sister, daughter, etc.

- Promote opportunities for valued roles such as co-worker, students, taxpayer, and citizen.

- Provide the support to build relationships between members of the local community who are not paid to be with the person.

- Seek out locations where the client's interests, culture, talent, and gifts can be shared with others with similar interests.

- Seek out housing and activities that are in areas convenient to a range of places to shop, bank, eat, worship, and learn in a natural environment.

- Advocate to end services which segregate persons with disabilities from natural, typical, and age appropriate activities available to other community members.

SECTION TWO

The Goal Writer's Resource Library: Prewritten Goals & Objectives

COMMUNICATION SKILLS

Assistance Objectives (To Maintain Skills)

&

Training Objectives (To Gain and Improve Upon Skills)

Browse a few innovative ideas.....

ASSISTANCE OBJECTIVES TO MAINTAIN COMMUNICATION SKILLS

- With assistance, __(name)__ will practice self-advocacy/communication skills by participation in the team satisfaction meeting _(# of trials)_ times a week. This is an assistance objective that will focus on participation in the skill area so that to maintain level of functioning. The objective will cease when __(name)__ no longer is interested or feels staff assistance necessary.

- With assistance, _(name)_ will access and utilize the computer _(# of trials)_ times a week. This is an assistance objective that will focus on participation in the skill area so that to maintain level of functioning. The objective will cease when _____(name) no longer is interested or feels staff assistance necessary.

- With assistance, __(name)__ will participate in conversational role-play to be able to use ordinary small-talk topics and responses _(# of trials)_ times a day. This is an assistance objective that will focus on participation in the skill area so that to maintain level of functioning. The objective will cease when __(name)__ no longer is interested or feels staff assistance necessary.

- With assistance, __(name)__ will practice simple introductions _(# of trials)_ times a day. This is an assistance objective that will focus on participation in the skill area so that to maintain level of functioning. The objective will cease when __(name)__ no longer is interested or feels staff assistance necessary.

- With assistance, __(name)__ will maintain her communication skills by participation in journal exercises _(# of trials)_ times a week. This is an assistance objective that will focus on participation in the skill area so that to maintain level of functioning. The objective will cease when __(name)__ no longer is interested or feels staff assistance necessary.

- With assistance, __(name)__ will record his/her thoughts and feelings in a journal _(# of trials)_ times a week. This is an assistance objective that will focus on participation in the skill area so that to maintain level of functioning. The objective will cease when __(name)__ no longer is interested or feels staff assistance necessary.

- With assistance, __(name)__ will learn to answer the telephone in an appropriate manner, _(# of trials)_ times per day/week. This is an assistance objective that will focus on participation in the skill area so that to maintain level of functioning. The objective will cease when __(name)__ no longer is interested or feels staff assistance necessary.

- With assistance, __(name)__ will dial a designated phone number, _(# of trials)_ times per (day/week). This is an assistance objective that will focus on the ability to correctly address this task and maintain skill level. The objective will cease when (name) no longer is interested or feels staff assistance necessary.

ASSISTANCE OBJECTIVES TO MAINTAIN COMMUNICATION SKILLS

- With staff assistance, __(name)__ will practice communication skills via email, _(# of trials)_ times per (day/week/or month). This is an assistance objective that will focus on participation in the skill area so that to maintain level of functioning. The objective will cease when __(name)__ no longer is interested or feels staff assistance necessary.

- With assistance, _(name)_ will list personal likes and interests _(# of trials)_ times per (day/week/or month). This is an assistance objective that will focus on participation in the skill area so that to maintain level of functioning. The objective will cease when __(name)__ no longer is interested or feels staff assistance necessary.

- With assistance, __(name)__ will indicate things that make him/her happy _(# of trials)_ times per (day/week/or month). This is an assistance objective that will focus on participation in the skill area so that to maintain level of functioning. The objective will cease when __(name)__ no longer is interested or feels staff assistance necessary.

- With assistance, __(name)__ will indicate things that make him/her sad and unhappy _(# of trials)_ times (day/week/or month). This is an assistance objective that will focus on participation in the skill area so that to maintain level of functioning. The objective will cease when __(name)__ no longer is interested or feels staff assistance necessary.

- With assistance, _(name)_ will communicate needs and wants _(# of trials)_ times per day. This is an assistance objective that will focus on participation in the skill area so that to maintain level of functioning. The objective will cease when __(name)__ no longer is interested or feels staff assistance necessary.

- With assistance, _(name)_ will practice identifying others by the correct name _(# of trials)_ times per day. This is an assistance objective that will focus on participation in the skill area so that to maintain level of functioning. The objective will cease when __(name)__ no longer is interested or feels staff assistance necessary.

- With staff assistance, _(name)_ will contact friends to participate in mutual enjoyable activities, _(# of trials)_ times per (day/week/or month). This is an assistance objective that will focus on participation in the skill area so that to maintain level of functioning. The objective will cease when __(name)__ no longer is interested or feels staff assistance necessary.

- With staff prompting, _(name)_ will utilize and maintain appropriate personal space while communicating with others, _(# of trials)_ times per day. This is an assistance objective that will focus on participation in the skill area so that to maintain level of functioning. The objective will cease when __(name)__ no longer is interested or feels staff assistance necessary.

ASSISTANCE OBJECTIVES TO MAINTAIN COMMUNICATION SKILLS

- With assistance, __(name)__ will utilize appropriate communication skills by directing conversation away from topics of preservation and repeatedly asked questions, __(# of trials)__ times per (day/week/or month). This is an assistance objective that will focus on participation in the skill area so that to maintain level of functioning. The objective will cease when __(name)__ no longer is interested or feels staff assistance necessary.

- With prompting, __(name)__ will verbally communicate with others by utilizing an audible tone, __(# of trials)__ times a day. This is an assistance objective that will focus on participation in the skill area so that to maintain level of functioning. The objective will cease when __(name)__ no longer is interested or feels staff assistance necessary.

- With prompting, __(name)__ will verbally communicate with others by lowering voice to appropriate limits, __(# of trials)__ times a day. This is an assistance objective that will focus on participation in the skill area so that to maintain level of functioning. The objective will cease when __(name)__ no longer is interested or feels staff assistance necessary.

- With prompting, __(name)__ will maintain eye contact with others while communicating __(# of trials)__ times per (day/week/or month). This is an assistance objective that will focus on participation in the skill area so that to maintain level of functioning. The objective will cease when __(name)__ no longer is interested or feels staff assistance necessary.

- With prompting, __(name)__ will utilize an appropriate communication style by refraining from socially inappropriate language, __(# of trials)__ times per (day/week/ or month). This is an assistance objective that will focus on participation in the skill area so that to maintain level of functioning. The objective will cease when __(name)__ no longer is interested or feels staff assistance necessary.

- With assistance, __(name)__ will order a desired food item from a cashier or wait staff, __(# of trials)__ times per (day/week/or month). This is an assistance objective that will focus on participation in the skill area so that to maintain level of functioning. The objective will cease when __(name)__ no longer is interested or feels staff assistance necessary.

- With prompting, __(name)__ will greet others with a handshake opposed to a hug, __(# of trials)__ times per (day/week/or month). This is an assistance objective that will focus on participation in the skill area so that to maintain level of functioning. The objective will cease when __(name)__ no longer is interested or feels staff assistance necessary.

- With prompting, __(name)__ will respond when spoken to or name is called, __(# of trials)__ times per day. This is an assistance objective that will focus on participation in the skill area so that to maintain level of functioning. The objective will cease when __(name)__ no longer is interested or feels staff assistance necessary.

Paul Spicer, QMRP

ASSISTANCE OBJECTIVES TO MAINTAIN COMMUNICATION SKILLS

- With assistance, __(name)__ will verbally state personal social security number, (# of trials) times per (day/week/or month). This is an assistance objective that will focus on participation in the skill area so that to maintain level of functioning. The objective will cease when __(name)__ no longer is interested or feels staff assistance necessary.

- With assistance, __(name)__ will write personal social security number, (# of trials) times per (day/week/or month). This is an assistance objective that will focus on participation in the skill area so that to maintain level of functioning. The objective will cease when __(name)__ no longer is interested or feels staff assistance necessary.

- With assistance, __(name)__ will verbally state home telephone number, (# of trials) times per (day/week/or month). This is an assistance objective that will focus on participation in the skill area so that to maintain level of functioning. The objective will cease when __(name)__ no longer is interested or feels staff assistance necessary.

- With assistance, __(name)__ will independently write home telephone number, (# of trials) times per (day/week/or month). This is an assistance objective that will focus on participation in the skill area so that to maintain level of functioning. The objective will cease when __(name)__ no longer is interested or feels staff assistance necessary.

- With assistance, __(name)__ will verbally state home address, (# of trials) times per (day/week/or month). This is an assistance objective that will focus on participation in the skill area so that to maintain level of functioning. The objective will cease when __(name)__ no longer is interested or feels staff assistance necessary.

- With assistance, __(name)__ will write home address, (# of trials) times per (day/week/or month). This is an assistance objective that will focus on participation in the skill area so that to maintain level of functioning. The objective will cease when __(name)__ no longer is interested or feels staff assistance necessary.

- With assistance, __(name)__ will verbally state correct birth date, (# of trials) times per (day/week/or month). This is an assistance objective that will focus on participation in the skill area so that to maintain level of functioning. The objective will cease when __(name)__ no longer is interested or feels staff assistance necessary.

- With assistance, __(name)__ will write the correct birth date, (# of trials) times per (day/week/or month). This is an assistance objective that will focus on participation in the skill area so that to maintain level of functioning. The objective will cease when __(name)__ no longer is interested or feels staff assistance necessary.

- With assistance, __(name)__ will practice communication skills by stating first and last name to a peer, (# of trials) times per (day/week/or month). This is an assistance objective that will focus on participation in the skill area so that to maintain level of functioning. The objective will cease when __(name)__ no longer is interested or feels staff assistance necessary.

Browse a few innovative ideas…..

TRAINING OBJECTIVES TO IMPROVE COMMUNICATION SKILLS

- Without prompting, _(name)_ will independently utilize communication/conversation techniques that are appropriate to time and place when conversing with others, _(# of trials)_ times a day. This is a training objective that will be considered complete when _(name)_ independently utilizes appropriate conversation to the time and place on _(#)_ consecutive trials.

- Without prompting, _(name)_ will independently utilize appropriate boundaries when communicating with others, _(# of trials)_ times per day. This is a training objective that will be complete when he/she has independently implemented appropriate boundaries on _(#)_ consecutive trials.

- Without prompting, _(name)_ will independently utilize appropriate communication skills by waiting before interrupting a conversation, _(# of trials)_ times per day. This is a training objective that will be considered complete when _(name)_ has successfully waited without interrupting conversations on _(#)_ consecutive trials.

- Without prompting, _(name)_ will independently utilize appropriate communication techniques by waiting for conversation to end before walking away, _(# of trials)_ times per day. This is a training objective that will be considered complete when he/she has completed the skill correctly on _(#)_ consecutive trials.

- Without assistance, _(name)_ will independently utilize appropriate boundaries while greeting friends and staff upon arrival to the program _(# of trials)_ times a day. This is a training objective that will be considered complete when _(name)_ independently completes the task on _(#)_ consecutive trials.

- Without assistance, _(name)_ will independently record his/her daily activities in a journal _(# of trials)_ times a week. This is a training objective that will focus on the ability to improve skill level and independence in this area. The objective will be considered complete when it is addressed independently on _(#)_ consecutive trials.

- Without prompting, _(name)_ will independently utilize the telephone in the proper fashion, _(# of trials)_ times per _(day/week/or month)_. This is a training objective that will focus on the ability to improve skill level and independence in this area. This objective will be considered complete when it is addressed independently in a correct fashion on _(#)_ consecutive trials.

- Without prompting, _(name)_ will independently utilize the correct name when addressing others, _(# of trials)_ times per day. This is a training objective that will focus on the ability to improve skill level and independence in this area. This objective will be considered complete when it is addressed independently on _(#)_ consecutive trials.

TRAINING OBJECTIVES TO IMPROVE COMMUNICATION SKILLS

- Without prompting, __(name)__ will independently utilize appropriate communication skills by directing conversation away from topics of preservation and repeatedly asked questions, __(# of trials)__ times per __(day/week/or month)__. This is a training objective that will be considered complete when he/she has independently addressed the task in an appropriate fashion on __(#)__ consecutive trials.

- Without prompting, __(name)__ will verbally communicate with others by utilizing an audible tone, __(# of trials)__ times a day. This is a training objective that will be considered complete when he/she has independently utilized an audible tone on __(#)__ consecutive trials.

- Without prompting, __(name)__ will verbally communicate with others by lowering voice to appropriate limits, __(# of trials)__ times a day. This is a training objective that will be considered complete when he/she has independently lowered voice level to appropriate limits on __(#)__ consecutive trials.

- Without prompting, __(name)__ will utilize eye contact with others while communicating __(# of trials)__ times per __(day/week/or month)__. This is a training objective that will be considered complete when the task has been completed independently, without prompting, on __(#)__ consecutive trials.

- Without prompting, __(name)__ will utilize an appropriate communication style by refraining from socially inappropriate language, __(# of trials)__ times per __(day/week/or month)__. This is a training objective that will be considered complete when he/she has independently utilized an appropriate communication style by refraining from offensive language on __(#)__ consecutive trials.

- Without assistance, __(name)__ will independently order a desired food item from a cashier or wait staff, __(# of trials)__ times per __(day/week/or month)__. This is a training objective that will be considered complete when the task has been addressed independently, without prompting, on __(#)__ consecutive trials.

- Without prompting, __(name)__ will independently greet others with a handshake opposed to a hug, __(# of trials)__ times per __(day/week/or month)__. This is a training objective that will be considered complete when the task has been addressed independently, without prompting, in a correct fashion on __(#)__ consecutive trials.

- Without prompting, __(name)__ will speak in complete sentences, __(# of trials)__ times per day. This is a training objective that will be considered complete when the skill has been addressed independently, without prompting, in a correct fashion on __(#)__ consecutive trials.

- Without prompting, __(name)__ will respond when spoken to or name is called, __(# of trials)__ times per day. This is a training objective that will be considered complete when the skill has been addressed independently, without prompting, in a correct fashion on __(#)__ consecutive trials.

TRAINING OBJECTIVES TO IMPROVE COMMUNICATION SKILLS

- Without assistance, __(name)__ will independently verbalize social security number, (# of trials) times per (day/week/or month). This is a training objective that will be considered complete when the correct social security number has been stated independently on _(#)___ consecutive trials.

- Without assistance, __(name)__ will independently write social security number, (# of trials) times per (day/week/or month). This is a training objective that will be considered complete when the correct social security number has been written independently on _(#)___ consecutive trials.

- Without assistance, __(name)__ will independently verbalize home telephone number, (# of trials) times per (day/week/or month). This is a training objective that will be considered complete when the correct telephone number has been stated independently on __(#)__ consecutive trials.

- Without assistance, __(name)__ will independently write home telephone number, (# of trials) times per (day/week/or month). This is a training objective that will be considered complete when the correct telephone number has been stated independently on _(#)__consecutive trials.

- Without assistance, __(name)__ will independently verbalize home address, (# of trials) times per (day/week/or month). This is a training objective that will be considered complete when the correct home address has been stated independently on __(#)_ _consecutive trials.

- Without assistance, __(name)__ will independently write home address, (# of trials) times per (day/week/or month). This is a training objective that will be considered complete when the correct home address has been written independently on __(#)_ _consecutive trials.

- Without assistance, __(name)__ will independently verbalize correct birth date, (# of trials) times per (day/week/or month). This is a training objective that will be considered complete when the correct birth date has been stated independently on __(#)___ consecutive trials.

- Without assistance, __(name)__ will independently write the correct birth date, (# of trials) times per (day/week/or month). This is a training objective that will be considered complete when the correct birth date has been independently written on __(#)___ consecutive trials.

- Without assistance, __(name)__ will independently perform verbal introductions by stating first and last name to a peer, (# of trials) times per (day/week/or month). This is a training objective that will be considered complete when the correct birth date has been independently written on __(#)___ consecutive trials.

SELF EXPLORATION & AWARENESS

Assistance Objectives (To Maintain Skills)

&

Training Objectives (To Gain and Improve Upon Skills)

Browse a few innovative ideas.....

ASSISTANCE OBJECTIVES TO MAINTAIN SELF-EXPLORATION & AWARENESS

- With assistance, __(name)__ will practice communication skills by participation in a group satisfaction meeting or organized group discussion _(# of trials)_ times a week. This is an assistance objective that will focus on participation in the skill area so that to maintain level of functioning. The objective will cease when __(name)__ no longer is interested or feels staff assistance necessary.

- With assistance, __(name)__ will maintain an anger diary, _(# of trials)_ times per (day, week, or month) . This is an assistance objective that will focus on participation in the skill area so that to maintain level of functioning. The objective will cease when __(name)__ no longer is interested or feels staff assistance necessary.

- With assistance, __(name)__ will indicate things that make him/her happy _(# of trials)_ times per (day, week, or month). This is an assistance objective that will focus on participation in the skill area so that to maintain level of functioning. The objective will cease when __(name)__ no longer is interested or feels staff assistance necessary.

- With assistance, __(name)__ will indicate things that make him/her sad and unhappy _(# of trials)_ times per (day, week, or month). This is an assistance objective that will focus on participation in the skill area so that to maintain level of functioning. The objective will cease when __(name)__ no longer is interested or feels staff assistance necessary.

- With assistance, __(name)__ will communicate needs and wants _(# of trials)_ times per day. This is an assistance objective that will focus on participation in the skill area so that to maintain level of functioning. The objective will cease when __(name)__ no longer is interested or feels staff assistance necessary.

- With assistance, __(name)__ will order a desired meal item from a cashier or wait staff, _(# of trials)_ times per (day/week/or month). This is an assistance objective that will focus on participation in the skill area so that to maintain level of functioning. The objective will cease when __(name)__ no longer is interested or feels staff assistance necessary.

- With assistance, __(name)__ will maintain his/her self-awareness skills by participation in journal exercises _(# of trials)_ per (day, week, or month). This is an assistance objective that will focus on participation in the skill area so that to maintain level of functioning. The objective will cease when __(name)__ no longer is interested or feels staff assistance necessary.

- With assistance, __(name)__ will participate in a group/team meeting _(# of trials)_ times a (day, week, or month). This is an assistance objective that will focus on participation in the skill area so that to maintain level of functioning. The objective will cease when __(name)__ no longer is interested or feels staff assistance necessary.

ASSISTANCE OBJECTIVES TO MAINTAIN SELF-EXPLORATION & AWARENESS

- With assistance, __(name)__ will list likes and interests __(# of trials)__ times per (day, week, or month). This is an assistance objective that will focus on participation in the skill area so that to maintain level of functioning. The objective will cease when __(name)__ no longer is interested or feels staff assistance necessary.

- With assistance, __(name)__ will indicate things that make him/her happy __(# of trials)__ times per (day, week, or month). This is an assistance objective that will focus on participation in the skill area so that to maintain level of functioning. The objective will cease when __(name)__ no longer is interested or feels staff assistance necessary.

- With assistance, __(name)__ will indicate things that make him/her sad and unhappy __(# of trials)__ times per (day, week, or month). This is an assistance objective that will focus on participation in the skill area so that to maintain level of functioning. The objective will cease when __(name)__ no longer is interested or feels staff assistance necessary.

- With assistance, __(name)__ will communicate needs and wants __(# of trials)__ times per day. This is an assistance objective that will focus on participation in the skill area so that to maintain level of functioning. The objective will cease when __(name)__ no longer is interested or feels staff assistance necessary.

- With staff assistance, __(name)__ will utilize the Internet to research topics of interest, __(# of trials)__ times per (day/week/or month). This is an assistance objective that will focus on participation in the skill area so that to maintain level of functioning. The objective will cease when __(name)__ no longer is interested or feels staff assistance necessary.

- With assistance, __(name)__ will utilize the public library to research topics of interest, __(# of trials)__ times per (day/week/or month). This is an assistance objective that will focus on participation in the skill area so that to maintain level of functioning. The objective will cease when __(name)__ no longer is interested or feels staff assistance necessary.

- With assistance, __(name)__ will review personal medications, side effects, and expected outcomes with staff, __(# of trials)__ times per (day, week, or month). This is an assistance objective that will focus on participation in the skill area so that to maintain level of functioning. The objective will cease when __(name)__ no longer is interested or feels staff assistance necessary.

- With assistance, __(name)__ will verbally state personal social security number, (# of trials) times per (day/week/or month). This is an assistance objective that will focus on participation in the skill area so that to maintain level of functioning. The objective will cease when __(name)__ no longer is interested or feels staff assistance necessary.

ASSISTANCE OBJECTIVES TO MAINTAIN SELF-EXPLORATION & AWARENESS

- With assistance, __(name)__ will write personal social security number, (# of trials) times per (day/week/or month). This is an assistance objective that will focus on participation in the skill area so that to maintain level of functioning. The objective will cease when __(name)__ no longer is interested or feels staff assistance necessary.

- With assistance, __(name)__ will verbally state home telephone number, (# of trials) times per (day/week/or month). This is an assistance objective that will focus on participation in the skill area so that to maintain level of functioning. The objective will cease when __(name)__ no longer is interested or feels staff assistance necessary.

- With assistance, __(name)__ will independently write home telephone number, (# of trials) times per (day/week/or month). This is an assistance objective that will focus on participation in the skill area so that to maintain level of functioning. The objective will cease when __(name)__ no longer is interested or feels staff assistance necessary.

- With assistance, __(name)__ will verbally state home address, (# of trials) times per (day/week/or month). This is an assistance objective that will focus on participation in the skill area so that to maintain level of functioning. The objective will cease when __(name)__ no longer is interested or feels staff assistance necessary.

- With assistance, __(name)__ will write home address, (# of trials) times per (day/week/or month). This is an assistance objective that will focus on participation in the skill area so that to maintain level of functioning. The objective will cease when __(name)__ no longer is interested or feels staff assistance necessary.

- With assistance, __(name)__ will verbally state correct birth date, (# of trials) times per (day/week/or month). This is an assistance objective that will focus on participation in the skill area so that to maintain level of functioning. The objective will cease when __(name)__ no longer is interested or feels staff assistance necessary.

- With assistance, __(name)__ will write the correct birth date, (# of trials) times per (day/week/or month). This is an assistance objective that will focus on participation in the skill area so that to maintain level of functioning. The objective will cease when __(name)__ no longer is interested or feels staff assistance necessary.

Browse a few innovative ideas.....

TRAINING OBJECTIVES TO IMPROVE SELF-EXPLORATION & AWARENESS

- Without assistance, ___(name)___ will improve upon self-exploration skills by independently completing journal entries _(# of trials)_ per _(day/week/ or month)_. This is a training objective that will be considered complete when _(name)_ has independently completed journal entries on __(#)__ consecutive trials.

- Without prompting, _(name)_ will independently participate in a group/team meeting _(# of trials)_ times per _(day, week, or month)_. This is a training objective that will be considered complete when _(name)_ has independently participated in group/team meetings on __(#)__ consecutive trials.

- Without assistance, _(name)_ will independently state personal likes and interests _(# of trials)_ times per _(day, week, or month)_. This is a training objective that will be considered complete when _(name)_ has independently stated likes and dislikes on __(#)__ consecutive trials.

- Without assistance, _(name)_ will independently indicate things that make him/her happy _(# of trials)_ times per _(day, week, or month)_. This is a training objective that will be considered complete when _(name)_ has independently indicated things that make him/her happy on __(#)__ consecutive trials.

- Without assistance, _(name)_ will independently indicate things that make him/her sad and unhappy _(# of trials)_ times per _(day, week, or month)_. This is a training objective that will be considered complete when _(name)_ has independently indicated things that make him/her sad on __(#)__ consecutive trials.

- Without assistance, _(name)_ will independently communicate needs and wants _(# of trials)_ times per day. This is a training objective that will be considered complete when _(name)_ has independently communicated needs and wants on __(#)__ consecutive trials.

- Without assistance, _(name)_ will independently utilize the Internet to explore topics of interest, _(# of trials)_ times per _(day/week/or month)_. This is a training objective that will be considered complete when _(name)_ has independently utilized the Internet to explore topics of interest on __(#)__ consecutive trials.

- Without assistance, _(name)_ will independently utilize the public library to explore topics of interest, _(# of trials)_ times per _(day/week/or month)_. This is a training objective that will be considered complete when _(name)_ has independently utilized the public library to explore topics of interests on __(#)__ consecutive trials.

TRAINING OBJECTIVES TO IMPROVE SELF-EXPLORATION & AWARENESS

- Without assistance, ___(name)___ will independently state the name of personal medications, side effects, and expected outcomes, _(# of trials)_ times per day. This is a training objective that will be considered complete when ___(name)___ has independently state the correct medications, side effects, and expected outcomes on ___(#)___ consecutive trials.

- Without assistance, ___(name)___ will independently verbalize social security number, (# of trials) times per (day/week/or month). This is a training objective that will be considered complete when the correct social security number has been stated independently on___(#)___consecutive trials.

- Without assistance, ___(name)___ will independently write social security number, (# of trials) times per (day/week/or month). This is a training objective that will be considered complete when the correct social security number has been written independently on___(#)___consecutive trials.

- Without assistance, ___(name)___ will independently verbalize home telephone number, (# of trials) times per (day/week/or month). This is a training objective that will be considered complete when the correct telephone number has been stated independently on___(#)___consecutive trials.

- Without assistance, ___(name)___ will independently write home telephone number, (# of trials) times per (day/week/or month). This is a training objective that will be considered complete when the correct telephone number has been stated independently on___(#)___consecutive trials.

- Without assistance, _(name)_ will independently verbalize home address, (# of trials) times per (day/week/or month). This is a training objective that will be considered complete when the correct home address has been stated independently on___(#)___consecutive trials.

- Without assistance, ___(name)___ will independently write home address, (# of trials) times per (day/week/or month). This is a training objective that will be considered complete when the correct home address has been written independently on___(#)___consecutive trials.

- Without assistance, ___(name)___ will independently verbalize correct birth date, (# of trials) times per (day/week/or month). This is a training objective that will be considered complete when the correct birth date has been stated independently on___(#)___consecutive trials.

- Without assistance, ___(name)___ will independently write the correct birth date, (# of trials) times per (day/week/or month). This is a training objective that will be considered complete when the correct birth date has been independently written on___(#)___consecutive trials.

PHYSICAL & MENTAL HEALTH

Assistance Objectives (To Maintain Skills)

&

Training Objectives (To Gain and Improve Upon Skills)

ASSISTANCE OBJECTIVES TO MAINTAIN PHYSICAL & MENTAL HEALTH

- With assistance, __(name)__ will participate in a form of exercise of his/her choosing, __(# of trials)__ times per (day/week/or month). This is an assistance objective that will focus on participation in the skill area so that to maintain functioning level. The objective will cease when __(name)__ no longer is interested or feels staff assistance necessary.

- With assistance, __(name)__ will participate in health and nutritional familiarization by reviewing educational materials with staff members, __(# of trials)__ times per (day/week/or month). This is an assistance objective that will focus on participation in the skill area so that to maintain level of functioning. The objective will cease when (name)__ no longer is interested or feels staff assistance necessary.

- With assistance, __(name)__ will practice stress/anger management techniques with staff members, __(# of trials)__ a day. This is an assistance objective that will focus on participation in the skill area so that to maintain level of functioning. The objective will cease when __(name)__ no longer is interested or feels staff assistance necessary.

- With assistance, __(name)__ will ride a stationary bicycle for twenty minutes, __(# of trials)__ per (day/week/or month). This is an assistance objective that will focus on participation in the skill area so that to maintain level of functioning. The objective will cease when __(name)__ no longer is interested or feels staff assistance necessary.

- With assistance, __(name)__ will plan nutritious snacks and meals that include the five basic food groups, __(# of trials)__ times per (day/week/or month). This is an assistance objective that will focus on participation in the skill area so that to maintain level of functioning. The objective will cease when __(name)__ no longer is interested or feels staff assistance necessary.

- With assistance, __(name)__ will participate in simple muscle stretching exercises __(# of trials)__ times per (day/week/or month). This is an assistance objective that will focus on participation in the skill area so that to maintain level of functioning. The objective will cease when __(name)__ no longer is interested or feels staff assistance necessary.

- With assistance, __(name)__ will demonstrate healthy living skills by following good oral hygiene __(# of trials)__ times per day. This is an assistance objective that will focus on participation in the skill area so that to maintain level of functioning. The objective will cease when __(name)__ no longer is interested or feels staff assistance necessary.

Paul Spicer, QMRP

ASSISTANCE OBJECTIVES TO MAINTAIN PHYSICAL & MENTAL HEALTH

- With staff assistance, __(name)__ will review the name, physical appearance, and side efforts of his/her medications __(# of trials)__ times per day. This is an assistance objective that will focus on participation in the skill area so that to maintain level of functioning. The objective will cease when __(name)__ no longer is interested or feels staff assistance necessary.

- With staff assistance, __(name)__ will place personal medications into a daily medication management container, __(# of trials)__ times per (day/week/or month). This is an assistance objective designed to familiarize __(name)__ with the organization on medications and correct administration time. The objective will focus on participation in the skill area so that to maintain level of functioning. The objective will cease when __(name)__ no longer is interested or feels staff assistance necessary.

- With prompting, __(name)__ will hold his/her head up while maneuvering to avoid falls and obstacles, __(# of trials)__ times per day. This is an assistance objective that will focus on participation in the skill area so that to maintain level of functioning. The objective will cease when __(name)__ no longer is interested or feels staff assistance necessary.

- With assistance, __(name)__ will seek out handrails, ramps, and elevators to utilize while maneuvering in the community, __(# of trials)__ times per (day/week/or month). This is an assistance objective that will focus on participation in the skill area so that to maintain level of functioning. The objective will cease when __(name)__ no longer is interested or feels staff assistance necessary.

- With assistance, __(name)__ will practice presenting ID/medical info card upon request, __(# of trials)__ times per (day/week/or month). This is an assistance objective that will focus on participation in the skill area so that to maintain level of functioning. The objective will cease when __(name)__ no longer is interested or feels staff assistance necessary.

- With staff assistance, __(name)__ will practice role-playing the manner in which one obtains telephone assistance in an emergency (911), __(# of trials)__ times per (day/week/or month). This is an assistance objective that will focus on participation in the skill area so that to maintain level of functioning. The objective will cease when __(name)__ no longer is interested or feels staff assistance necessary.

- With assistance, __(name)__ will practice appropriate safety skills when handling sharp objects (knives, scissors, etc) on a daily basis. This is an assistance objective that will focus on participation in the skill area so that to maintain level of functioning. The objective will cease when __(name)__ no longer is interested or feels staff assistance necessary.

ASSISTANCE OBJECTIVES TO MAINTAIN PHYSICAL & MENTAL HEALTH

- With assistance,___(name)___ will practice appropriate health/safety skills by demonstrating knowledge of proper food storage, _(# of trials)_ times per (day/ week/or month). This is an assistance objective that will focus on participation in the skill area so that to maintain level of functioning. The objective will cease when (name)__ no longer is interested or feels staff assistance necessary.

- With assistance,_(name)_ will practice appropriate safety skills by correctly utilizing basic appliances, _(# of trials)_ times per (day/week/or month). This is an assistance objective that will focus on participation in the skill area so that to maintain level of functioning. The objective will cease when __(name)__ no longer is interested or feels staff assistance necessary.

- With assistance, _(name)__ will practice an understanding of basic safety signs (caution, danger, poison, exit, wet floor, warning), _(# of trials)_ times per (day/ week/or month). This is an assistance objective that will focus on participation in the skill area so that to maintain level of functioning. The objective will cease when (name)__ no longer is interested or feels staff assistance necessary.

- With assistance, _(name)_ will practice identifying emergency from non-emergency situations, _(# of trials)_ times per (day/week/or month). This is an assistance objective that will focus on participation in the skill area so that to maintain level of functioning. The objective will cease when __(name)__ no longer is interested or feels staff assistance necessary.

Browse a few innovative ideas.....

TRAINING OBJECTIVES TO IMPROVE PHYSICAL & MENTAL HEALTH

- Without prompting, __(name)__ will utilize his/her cane in a safe fashion by correctly performing a sweeping motion while mobilizing, __(# of trials)__ times a day. This is a training objective that will be considered complete when __(name)__ completes the task independently, without prompting, on __(#)__ consecutive trials.

- Without prompting, __(name)__ will utilize his/her walker in the correct fashion, __(# of trials)__ times a day. This is a training objective that will be considered complete when __(name)__ independently utilizes the walker correctly on __(#)__ consecutive trials.

- Without assistance, __(name)__ will independently look both ways before crossing the street/parking lot, __(# of trials)__ times a day. This is a training objective that will be considered complete when __(name)__ looks both ways, without prompting, on __(#)__ consecutive trials.

- Without prompting, __(name)__ will implement community safety precautions, __(# of trials)__ times per day. This is a training objective that will be considered complete when he/she addresses community safety precautions in an appropriate fashion on __(#)__ consecutive trials.

- Without assistance, __(name)__ will independently buckle his/her safety belt when riding in vehicles, __(# of trials)__ times a day. This is a training objective that will be considered complete when he/she independently buckles the safety belt, without prompting, on __(#)__ consecutive trials.

- Without assistance, __(name)__ will follow nutritious eating habits by preparing meals that include the five basic food groups, __(# of trials)__ times a week. This is a training objective that will be considered complete when he/she independently follows nutritious eating habits, without prompting, on __(#)__ consecutive trials.

- Without prompting, __(name)__ will demonstrate healthy living skills by following good oral hygiene, __(# of trials)__ times per day. This is a training objective that will be considered complete when independently addressed on __(#)__ consecutive trials.

- Without prompting, __(name)__ will state his/her health information and current medications, __(# of trials)__ times per (day/week/or month). This is a training objective that will be considered complete when __(name)__ independently completes the task in a correct fashion on __(#)__ consecutive trials.

- Without prompting, __(name)__ will identify the correct time to administer his/her medications, __(# of trials)__ per day. This is a training objective that will be considered complete when the correct time for medication delivery is independently selected on __(#)__ consecutive trials.

TRAINING OBJECTIVES TO IMPROVE PHYSICAL & MENTAL HEALTH

- Without assistance, __(name)__ will state the name of his personal medications __(# of trials)__ times per __(day/week/or month)__ This is a training objective that will be considered complete when the task has been completed independently, without prompting, in a correct fashion on __(#)__ consecutive trials.

- Without prompting, __(name)__ will independently initiate and engage in a physical exercise routine of his/her choice __(# of trials)__ times per __(day/week/or month)__. This is a training objective that will be considered complete when the exercise routine has been independently addressed on __(#)__ consecutive trials.

- Without prompting, __(name)__ will independently hold his/her head up while maneuvering to avoid falls and obstacles, __(# of trials)__ times per day. This is a training objective that will be considered complete when the skill has been addressed independently, without prompting, on __(#)__ consecutive trials.

- Without prompting, __(name)__ will seek out handrails, ramps, and elevators to utilize while maneuvering in the community, __(# of trials)__ times per __(day/week/or month)__. This is a training objective that is designed to improve independence with this particular skill. This is a training objective that will be considered complete when the task has been performed independently, without prompting, on __(#)__ consecutive trials.

- Upon request, __(name)__ will independently present I.D./Medical Info. Card, __(# of trials)__ times per __(day/week/or month)__. This is a training objective that will be considered complete when the skill has been addressed independently, without prompting, on __(#)__ consecutive trials.

- Upon request, __(name)__ will independently state the appropriate manner in which to receive telephone assistance when in an emergency (911), __(# of trials)__ times per __(day/week/or month)__. This is a training objective that will be considered complete when the appropriate response has been stated independently, without assistance, on __(#)__ consecutive trials.

- Without assistance, __(name)__ will independently demonstrate appropriate food handling skills, __(# of trials)__ times per __(day/week/or month)__. This is a training objective that will be considered complete when the skill has been addressed independently, without prompting, on __(#)__ consecutive trials.

- Without prompting, __(name)__ will demonstrate appropriate safety skills by refraining from touching hot surfaces while cooking, __(# of trials)__ times per day. This is a training objective that will be considered complete when the skill has been addressed independently, without prompting, on __(#)__ consecutive trials.

- Without prompting, __(name)__ will demonstrate appropriate safety skills by correctly handling sharp objects (knives, scissors, etc), __(# of trials)__ times per day. This is a training objective that will be considered complete when the skill has been addressed independently, without prompting, on __(#)__ consecutive trials.

TRAINING OBJECTIVES TO IMPROVE PHYSICAL & MENTAL HEALTH

- Without prompting,__(name)__ will demonstrate appropriate health/safety skills by demonstrating knowledge of proper food storage, _(# of trials)_ times per day. This is a training objective that will be considered complete when the skill has been addressed independently, without prompting, on __(#)__ consecutive trials.

- Without prompting,_(name)_ will demonstrate appropriate safety skills while utilizing basic appliances, _(# of trials)_ times per day. This is a training objective that will be considered complete when the skill has been addressed independently, without prompting, on __(#)__ consecutive trials.

- Without prompting,__(name)__ will demonstrate an understanding of basic safety signs (caution, danger, poison, exit, wet floor, warning), _(# of trials)_ times per day. This is a training objective that will be considered complete when the skill has been addressed independently, without prompting, on __(#)__ consecutive trials.

- Without prompting,__(name)__ will demonstrate the understanding of emergency from non-emergency situations, _(# of trials)_ times per (day/week/or month). This is a training objective that will be considered complete when the skill has been addressed independently, without prompting, on __(#)__ consecutive trials.

ACTIVITIES OF DAILY LIVING

Assistance Objectives (To Maintain Skills)

&

Training Objectives (To Gain and Improve Upon Skills)

ASSISTANCE OBJECTIVES TO MAINTAIN ACTIVITIES OF DAILY LIVING

- With assistance, __(name)__ will practice prioritizing the week's events through the use of a personal planner _(# of trials)_ times a (day/week/or month). This is an assistance objective that will focus on participation in the skill area so that to maintain level of functioning. The objective will cease when __(name)__ no longer is interested or feels staff assistance necessary.

- With assistance, __(name)__ will develop an activity calendar, _(# of trials)_ times per (day/week/or month). This is an assistance objective that will focus on participation in the skill area so that to maintain level of functioning. The objective will cease when __(name)__ no longer is interested or feels staff assistance necessary.

- With assistance, __(name)__ will plan a simple meal _(# of trials)_ times a (day/week/or month). This is an assistance objective that will focus on participation in the skill area so that to maintain level of functioning. The objective will cease when __(name)__ no longer is interested or feels staff assistance necessary.

- With assistance, __(name)__ will practice meal/menu planning by flipping through a cookbook and pointing to meal options of choice, _(# of trials)_ times a day. This is an assistance objective that will focus on participation in the skill area so that to maintain level of functioning. The objective will cease when __(name)__ no longer is interested or feels staff assistance necessary.

- With assistance, __(name)__ will prepare a grocery list _(# of trials)_ times per (day/week/or month). This is an assistance objective that will focus on participation in the skill area so that to maintain level of functioning. The objective will cease when (name)__ no longer is interested or feels staff assistance necessary.

- With assistance, __(name)__ will throw his/her trash away after eating, _(# of trials)_ times per (day/week/or month). This is an assistance objective that will focus on participation in the skill area so that to maintain level of functioning. The objective will cease when __(name)__ no longer is interested or feels staff assistance necessary.

- With assistance, __(name)__ will load the dishwasher, _(# of trials)_ times per (day/week/or month). This is an assistance objective that will focus on participation in the skill area so that to maintain level of functioning. The objective will cease when (name)__ no longer is interested or feels staff assistance necessary.

- With assistance, __(name)__ will utilize the correct amount of dishwashing detergent when operating the dishwasher, _(# of trials)_ times per (day/week/or month). This is an assistance objective that will focus on participation in the skill area so that to maintain level of functioning. The objective will cease when __(name)__ no longer is interested or feels staff assistance necessary.

ASSISTANCE OBJECTIVES TO MAINTAIN ACTIVITIES OF DAILY LIVING

- With assistance, __(name)__ will locate a predetermined item at the grocery store __(# of trials)__ times per (day/week/or month). This is an assistance objective that will focus on participation in the skill area so that to maintain level of functioning. The objective will cease when __(name)__ no longer is interested or feels staff assistance necessary.

- With assistance, __(name)__ will feed self, __(# of trials)__ times per day. This is an assistance objective that will focus on participation in the skill area so that to maintain level of functioning. The objective will cease when __(name)__ no longer is interested or feels staff assistance necessary.

- With assistance, __(name)__ will cut food items with a fork and knife, __(# of trials)__ times per day. This is an assistance objective that will focus on participation in the skill area so that to maintain level of functioning. The objective will cease when __(name)__ no longer is interested or feels staff assistance necessary.

- With prompting, __(name)__ will take small bites and chew food slowly, __(# of trials)__ times per day. This is an assistance objective that will focus on participation in the skill area so that to maintain level of functioning. The objective will cease when __(name)__ no longer is interested or feels staff assistance necessary.

Browse a few innovative ideas.....

TRAINING OBJECTIVES TO IMPROVE ACTIVITIES OF DAILY LIVING

- Without assistance, ___(name)___ will independently prepare a simple lunch _(# of trials)_ times a day. This is a training objective that will be considered met when (name)___ performs this task independently, without prompting or assistance, on ___(#)___ consecutive trials.

- Without prompting, ___(name)___ will independently wipe down the table after eating _(# of trials)_ a day. This is a training objective that will be considered complete when she performs this task independently on ___(#)___ consecutive trials.

- Without prompting, ___(name)___ will independently wash his/her hands before eating _ _(# of trials)_ times a day. This is a training objective that will be considered complete when ___(name)___ independently completes this task on ___(#)___ consecutive trials.

- Without assistance, ___(name)___ will develop an activity schedule that incorporates interests and hobbies _(# of trials)_ times per _(day/week/or month)_. This is a training objective that will be met when ___(name)___ independently develops an activity schedule without prompting on ___(#)___ consecutive trials.

- Without prompting, ___(name)___ will follow a personal planner of the day's events _(# of trials)_ times a day. This is a training objective that will be met when the planner is independently followed, without prompting, on ___(#)___ consecutive trials.

- Without assistance, ___(name)___ will develop a menu for a simple meal _(# of trials)_ times per _(day/week/or month)_. This is a training objective that will focus on _(name)_ ability to independently develop a menu, without prompting, on ___(#)___ consecutive trials.

- Without assistance, ___(name)___ will prepare a grocery list _(# of trials)_ times per _(day/week/or month)_. This is a training objective that will focus on the ability to address this skill independently. The objective will be considered complete when the task is addressed independently, without prompting, on ___(#)___ consecutive trials.

- Without prompting, ___(name)___ will remember to initiate a household chore routine, _(# of trials)_ times per _(day/week/or month)_. This is a training objective that will focus on the ability to independently initiate chores on _(#)_ consecutive trials.

- Without prompting, ___(name)___ will independently keep his/her room clean and tidy, by initiating room maintenance _(# of trials)_ times per _(day/week/or month)_. This is a training objective that will focus on the ability to independently initiate room maintenance on ___(#)___ consecutive trials.

- Without prompting, ___(name)___ will load the dishwasher, _(# of trials)_ times per _(day/week/or month)_. This is a training objective that will be considered complete when the task has been addressed independently on ___(#)___ consecutive trials.

TRAINING OBJECTIVES TO IMPROVE ACTIVITIES OF DAILY LIVING

- Without prompting, _(name)_ will utilize the correct amount of dishwashing detergent when operating the dishwasher, _(# of trials)_ times per _(day/week/or month)_. This is a training objective that will be considered complete when the task has been addressed independently on __(#)__ consecutive trials.

- Without assistance, _(name)_ will locate a predetermined item at the grocery store _(# of trials)_ times per _(day/week/or month)_. This is a training objective that will be considered complete when the task is completed correctly on _(#)_ consecutive trials.

- Without assistance, (name) will independently pour from one container to another cup or container, _(# of trials)_ times per day. This is a training objective that will be considered complete when the task has been addressed correctly, in an independent fashion, on __(#)__ consecutive trials.

- Without assistance, _(name)_ will independently feed self, _(# of trials)_ times per day. This is a training objective that will be considered complete when the task has been addressed correctly, in an independent fashion, on __(#)__ consecutive trials.

- Without assistance, _(name)_ will independently cut food items with a fork and knife, _(# of trials)_ times per day. This is a training objective that will be considered complete when the task has been addressed correctly, in an independent fashion, on __(#)__ consecutive trials.

- Without prompting, _(name)_ will independently take small bites and chew food slowly, _(# of trials)_ times per day. This is a training objective that will be considered complete when the task has been addressed correctly, in an independent fashion, on __(#)__ consecutive trials.

PERSONAL HYGIENE

Assistance Objectives (To Maintain Skills)

&

Training Objectives (To Gain and Improve Upon Skills)

Browse a few innovative ideas.....

ASSISTANCE OBJECTIVES TO MAINTAIN PERSONAL HYGIENE SKILLS

- With assistance, __(name)__ will complete toileting skills _(# of trials)_ times per day. This is an assistance objective designed so that the skill can be addressed and maintained. This is an assistance objective that will focus on participation in the skill area so that to maintain level of functioning. The objective will cease when __(name)__ no longer is interested or feels staff assistance necessary.

- With assistance, __(name)__ will correctly brush his/her teeth, _(# of trials)_ times a day. This is an assistance objective that will focus on participation in the skill area so that to maintain level of functioning. The objective will cease when __(name)__ no longer is interested or feels staff assistance necessary.

- With assistance, __(name)__ will squeeze the appropriate amount of toothpaste onto the brush bristles, _(# of trials)_ times a day. This is an assistance objective that will focus on participation in the skill area so that to maintain level of functioning. The objective will cease when __(name)__ no longer is interested or feels staff assistance necessary.

- With assistance, __(name)__ will shop for personal hygiene supplies _(# of trials)_ times per _(day/week/or month)_. This is an assistance objective that will focus on participation in the skill area so that to maintain level of functioning. The objective will cease when __(name)__ no longer is interested or feels staff assistance necessary.

- With assistance, __(name)__ will brush his/her hair in an appropriate fashion, _(# of trials)_ times per day. This is an assistance objective that will focus on participation in the skill area so that to maintain level of functioning. The objective will cease when __(name)__ no longer is interested or feels staff assistance necessary.

- With assistance, __(name)__ will perform nail care in an appropriate fashion, _(# of trials)_ per _(day/week/or month)_. This is an assistance objective that will focus on participation in the skill area so that to maintain level of functioning. The objective will cease when __(name)__ no longer is interested or feels staff assistance necessary.

- With assistance, __(name)__ will apply the appropriate amount of hand cream, _(# of trials)_ per day. This is an assistance objective designed so that the skill will be addressed and maintained. This is an assistance objective that will focus on participation in the skill area so that to maintain level of functioning. The objective will cease when __(name)__ no longer is interested or feels staff assistance necessary.

- With assistance, __(name)__ will wash his/her hands after using the bathroom _(# of trials)_ times a day. This is an assistance objective that will focus on participation in the skill area so that to maintain level of functioning. The objective will cease when __(name)__ no longer is interested or feels staff assistance necessary.

ASSISTANCE OBJECTIVES TO MAINTAIN PERSONAL HYGIENE SKILLS

- With prompting, __(name)__ will utilize the correct water temperature (warm soapy water) when washing hands, _(# of trials)_ times per day. This is an assistance objective that will focus on participation in the skill area so that to maintain level of functioning. The objective will cease when __(name)__ no longer is interested or feels staff assistance necessary.

- With assistance, __(name)__ will independently dry hands in an appropriate fashion, _(# of trials)_ times per day. This is an assistance objective that will focus on participation in the skill area so that to maintain level of functioning. The objective will cease when __(name)__ no longer is interested or feels staff assistance necessary.

- With assistance, __(name)__ will fasten and adjust clothing after toileting, _(# of trials)_ times per day. This is an assistance objective that will focus on participation in the skill area so that to maintain level of functioning. The objective will cease when __(name)__ no longer is interested or feels staff assistance necessary.

- With assistance, __(name)__ will put on and remove elastic waist garments, _(# of trials)_ times per day. This is an assistance objective that will focus on participation in the skill area so that to maintain level of functioning. The objective will cease when __(name)__ no longer is interested or feels staff assistance is necessary.

Browse a few innovative ideas.....

TRAINING OBJECTIVES TO IMPROVE PERSONAL HYGIENE SKILLS

- Without prompting, __(name)__ will independently follow a toileting routine _(# of trials)_ times a day. This is a training objective that will be considered complete when __(name)__ independently follows this routine, without prompting, on ___(#)___ consecutive trials.

- Without assistance, __(name)__ will complete toileting skills _(# of trials)_ times per day. This is a training objective designed so that __(name)__ will improve independence level when addressing toileting skills. This objective will be considered complete when the task is addressed independently, without prompting, on __(#)__ consecutive trials.

- Without prompting, __(name)__ will independently wash his/her hands after using the bathroom _(# of trials)_ times a day. This is a training objective that will be considered complete when __(name)__ independently performs the task, without prompting, on __(#)__ consecutive trials.

- Without prompting, __(name)__ will independently utilize the correct water temperature (warm soapy water) when washing hands, _(# of trials)_ times per day. This is a training objective that will be considered complete when __(name)__ independently performs the task, without prompting, in a correct fashion on __(#)__ consecutive trials.

- Without prompting, __(name)__ will independently dry hands in an appropriate fashion, _(# of trials)_ times per day. This is a training objective that will be considered complete when __(name)__ independently performs the task, without prompting, in a correct fashion on __(#)__ consecutive trials.

- Without prompting, __(name)__ will independently wash his/her face after eating _(# of trials)_ times a day. This is a training objective that will be considered complete when __(name)__ independently performs the task on __(#)__ consecutive trials.

- Without prompting, __(name)__ will wipe his/her eyeglasses clean _(# of trials)_ times per _(day/week/or month)_. This is a training objective that will be considered complete when __(name)__ independently performs the task on __(#)__ consecutive trials.

- Without prompting, __(name)__ will independently remember to brush his/her teeth _ _(# of trials)_ times a day. This is a training objective that will be considered complete when __(name)__ independently completes this task on __(#)__ consecutive trials.

- Without prompting, __(name)__ will independently brush all four quadrants of the mouth in a correct fashion _(# of trials)_ times a day. This is a training objective that will be considered met when the task is completed independently in a correct on __(#)__ consecutive trials.

TRAINING OBJECTIVES TO IMPROVE PERSONAL HYGIENE SKILLS

- Without prompting, ___(name)___ will independently place the correct amount of toothpaste onto the brush bristles, _(# of trials)_ times a day. This is a training objective that will be considered complete when the task is addressed independently on ___(#)___ consecutive trials.

- Without prompting, ___(name)___ will brush his/her hair in an appropriate fashion, _(# of trials)_ times per day. This is a training objective designed so that the skill will be improved upon. The objective will be considered complete when it has been addressed independently, without prompting, on ___(#)___ consecutive trials.

- Without prompting, ___(name)___ will perform nail care in an appropriate fashion, _(# of trials)_ times per (day/week/or month). This is a training objective designed so that the skill will be improved upon. The objective will be considered complete when it has been addressed independently, without prompting, on ___(#)___ consecutive trials.

- Without prompting, (name) will apply the appropriate amount of hand cream, _(# of trials)_ per day. This is a training objective that will be considered complete when the task has been addressed independently in an appropriate fashion on ___(#)___ consecutive trials.

- Without prompting, ___(name)___ will independently demonstrate appropriate eating etiquette _(# of trials)_ times per day. This is a training objective that will be considered complete when the task has been addressed independently in an appropriate fashion on ___(#)___ consecutive trials.

- Without prompting, ___(name)___ will purchase personal hygiene supplies needed for a healthy hygiene routine, _(# of trials)_ per (day/week/or month). This is a training objective that will be considered complete when he/she completes the objective independently on ___(#)___ consecutive trials.

- Without assistance, ___(name)___ will put on and remove elastic waist garments, _(# of trials)_ per (day/week/or month). This is a training objective that will be considered complete when the task has been addressed independently in an appropriate fashion on ___(#)___ consecutive trials.

- Without prompting , ___(name)___ will indicate wet or soiled pants by vocalizing to staff, _(# of trials)_ per (day/week/or month). This is a training objective that will be considered complete when the task is completed independently, without prompting, on ___(#)___ consecutive trials.

- Without assistance, ___(name)___ will fasten and adjust clothing after toileting, _(# of trials)_ per (day/week/or month). This is a training objective that will be considered complete when the task has been addressed independently in an appropriate fashion on ___(#)___ consecutive trials.

STRESS MANAGEMENT

Assistance Objectives (To Maintain Skills)

&

Training Objectives (To Gain and Improve Upon Skills)

Browse a few innovative ideas......

ASSISTANCE OBJECTIVES TO MAINTAIN STRESS MANAGEMENT SKILLS

- With assistance, __(name)__ will practice managing physical aggression by removing self from stressful stimuli when agitated. The objective will be addressed on a daily basis. This is an assistance objective that will focus on participation in the skill area so that to maintain level of functioning. The objective will cease when __(name)__ no longer is interested or feels staff assistance necessary.

- With assistance, __(name)__ will practice managing physical aggression by implementing deep breathing techniques when agitated. The objective will be addressed on a daily basis. This is an assistance objective that will focus on participation in the skill area so that to maintain level of functioning. The objective will cease when __(name)__ no longer is interested or feels staff assistance is necessary.

- With assistance, __(name)__ will practice managing physical aggression by implementing positive self-talk and imagery when agitated. The objective will be addressed on a daily basis. This is an assistance objective that will focus on participation in the skill area so that to maintain level of functioning. The objective will cease when __(name)__ no longer is interested or feels staff assistance necessary.

- With assistance, __(name)__ will practice managing physical aggression by implementing an exercise routine when agitated. The objective will be addressed on a daily basis. This is an assistance objective that will focus on participation in the skill area so that to maintain level of functioning. The objective will cease when __(name)__ no longer is interested or feels staff assistance necessary.

- With assistance, __(name)__ will practice managing physical aggression by seeking out peers or staff to talk to when agitated. The objective will be addressed on a daily basis. This is an assistance objective that will focus on participation in the skill area so that to maintain level of functioning. The objective will cease when __(name)__ no longer is interested or feels staff assistance necessary.

- With assistance, __(name)__ will practice managing verbal aggression by removing self from stressful stimuli when agitated. The objective will be addressed on a daily basis. This is an assistance objective that will focus on participation in the skill area so that to maintain level of functioning. The objective will cease when __(name)__ no longer is interested or feels staff assistance necessary.

- With assistance, __(name)__ will practice managing verbal aggression by implementing deep breathing techniques when agitated. The objective will be addressed on a daily basis. This is an assistance objective that will focus on participation in the skill area so that to maintain level of functioning. The objective will cease when __(name)__ no longer is interested or feels staff assistance necessary.

ASSISTANCE OBJECTIVES TO MAINTAIN STRESS MANAGEMENT SKILLS

- With assistance, _(name)_ will practice managing verbal aggression by implementing positive self-talk and imagery when agitated. The objective will be addressed on a daily basis. This is an assistance objective that will focus on participation in the skill area so that to maintain level of functioning. The objective will cease when _(name)_ no longer is interested or feels staff assistance necessary.

- With assistance, _(name)_ will practice managing verbal aggression by implementing an exercise routine when agitated. The objective will be addressed on a daily basis. This is an assistance objective that will focus on participation in the skill area so that to maintain level of functioning. The objective will cease when _(name)_ no longer is interested or feels staff assistance necessary.

- With assistance, _(name)_ will practice managing verbal aggression by seeking out peers or staff to talk to when agitated. The objective will be addressed on a daily basis. This is an assistance objective that will focus on participation in the skill area so that to maintain level of functioning. The objective will cease when _(name)_ no longer is interested or feels staff assistance is necessary.

- With assistance, _(name)_ will practice managing self-abusive behavior by removing self from stressful stimuli when agitated. The objective will be addressed on a daily basis. This is an assistance objective that will focus on participation in the skill area so that to maintain level of functioning. The objective will cease when _(name)_ no longer is interested or feels staff assistance necessary.

- With assistance, _(name)_ will practice managing self-abusive behavior by implementing deep breathing techniques when agitated. The objective will be addressed on a daily basis. This is an assistance objective that will focus on participation in the skill area so that to maintain level of functioning. The objective will cease when _(name)_ no longer is interested or feels staff assistance necessary.

- With assistance, _(name)_ will practice managing self-abusive behavior by implementing positive self-talk and imagery when agitated. The objective will be addressed on a daily basis. This is an assistance objective that will focus on participation in the skill area so that to maintain level of functioning. The objective will cease when _(name)_ no longer is interested or feels staff assistance necessary.

- With assistance, _(name)_ will practice managing self-abusive behavior by implementing an exercise routine when agitated. The objective will be addressed on a daily basis. This is an assistance objective that will focus on participation in the skill area so that to maintain level of functioning. The objective will cease when _(name)_ no longer is interested or feels staff assistance necessary.

- With assistance, _(name)_ will practice managing self-abusive behavior by seeking out peers and staff to talk to when agitated. The objective will be addressed on a daily basis. This is an assistance objective that will focus on participation in the skill area so that to maintain level of functioning. The objective will cease when _(name)_ no longer is interested or feels staff assistance necessary.

ASSISTANCE OBJECTIVES TO MAINTAIN STRESS MANAGEMENT SKILLS

- With assistance, __(name)__ will practice managing sexual behavior by restraining from inappropriate displays of affection. The objective will be addressed on a daily basis. This is an assistance objective that will focus on participation in the skill area so that to maintain level of functioning. The objective will cease when __(name)__ no longer is interested or feels staff assistance necessary.

- With assistance, __(name)__ will practice managing destructive behavior by refraining from destroying property. The objective will be addressed on a daily basis. This is an assistance objective that will focus on participation in the skill area so that to maintain level of functioning. The objective will cease when __(name)__ no longer is interested or feels staff assistance necessary.

- With assistance, __(name)__ will practice respecting the property of others by refraining from taking property that belongs to someone else. The objective will be addressed on a daily basis. This is an assistance objective that will focus on participation in the skill area so that to maintain level of functioning. The objective will cease when __(name)__ no longer is interested or feels staff assistance necessary.

- With assistance, __(name)__ will practice self-control by weighing consequences of actions before making decisions. The objective will be addressed on a daily basis. This is an assistance objective that will focus on participation in the skill area so that to maintain level of functioning. The objective will cease when __(name)__ no longer is interested or feels staff assistance necessary.

- With assistance, __(name)__ will practice managing repetitive behavior by demonstrating self-control. The objective will be addressed on a daily basis. This is an assistance objective that will focus on participation in the skill area so that to maintain level of functioning. The objective will cease when __(name)__ no longer is interested or feels staff assistance necessary.

- With assistance, __(name)__ will practice managing repetitive behavior by refraining from excessive preoccupation with objects. The objective will be addressed on a daily basis. This is an assistance objective that will focus on participation in the skill area so that to maintain level of functioning. The objective will cease when __(name)__ no longer is interested or feels staff assistance necessary.

- With assistance, __(name)__ will practice remaining focused on a specific activity for extended periods of time. The objective will be addressed on a daily basis. This is an assistance objective that will focus on participation in the skill area so that to maintain level of functioning. The objective will cease when __(name)__ no longer is interested or feels staff assistance necessary.

- With assistance, __(name)__ will practice remaining focused on a specific activity with others for an allotted amount of time. The objective will be addressed on a daily basis. This is an assistance objective that will focus on participation in the skill area so that to maintain level of functioning. The objective will cease when __(name)__ no longer is interested or feels staff assistance necessary.

ASSISTANCE OBJECTIVES TO MAINTAIN STRESS MANAGEMENT SKILLS

- With assistance, ___(name)___ will practice refraining from dangerous behaviors by refraining from eating or putting non-edible items in mouth. The objective will be addressed on a daily basis. This is an assistance objective that will focus on participation in the skill area so that to maintain level of functioning. The objective will cease when ___(name)___ no longer is interested or feels staff assistance necessary.

- With assistance, ___(name)___ will practice refraining from hording behaviors by refraining from collecting inappropriate amounts of food and/or objects. The objective will be addressed on a daily basis. This is an assistance objective that will focus on participation in the skill area so that to maintain level of functioning. The objective will cease when ___(name)___ no longer is interested or feels staff assistance necessary.

Browse a few innovative ideas.....

TRAINING OBJECTIVES TO IMPROVE STRESS MANAGEMENT SKILLS

- Without prompting, __(name)__ will independently manage physical aggression by removing self from stressful stimuli, __(# of trials)__ per __(day)__. This is a training objective that will be considered complete when __(name)__ independently completes the task on __(#)__ consecutive trials.

- Without prompting, __(name)__ will independently manage physical aggression by implementing deep breathing techniques when agitated, __(# of trials)__ per __(day)__. This is a training objective that will be considered complete when __(name)__ independently completes the task on __(#)__ consecutive trials.

- Without prompting, __(name)__ will independently manage physical aggression by implementing positive self-talk and imagery when agitated, __(# of trials)__ per __(day)__. This is a training objective that will be considered complete when __(name)__ independently completes the task on __(#)__ consecutive trials.

- Without prompting, __(name)__ will independently manage physical aggression by implementing an exercise routine when agitated, __(# of trials)__ per __(day)__. This is a training objective that will be considered complete when __(name)__ independently completes the task on __(#)__ consecutive trials.

- Without prompting, __(name)__ will independently manage physical aggression by seeking out peers or staff to talk to when agitated, __(# of trials)__ per __(day)__. This is a training objective that will be considered complete when __(name)__ independently completes the task on __(#)__ consecutive trials.

- Without prompting, __(name)__ will independently manage verbal aggression by removing self from stressful stimuli when agitated, __(# of trials)__ per __(day)__. This is a training objective that will be considered complete when __(name)__ independently completes the task on __(#)__ consecutive trials.

- Without prompting, __(name)__ will independently manage verbal aggression by implementing deep breathing techniques when agitated, __(# of trials)__ per __(day)__. This is a training objective that will be considered complete when __(name)__ independently completes the task on __(#)__ consecutive trials.

- Without prompting, __(name)__ will independently manage verbal aggression by implementing positive self-talk and imagery when agitated, __(# of trials)__ per __(day)__. This is a training objective that will be considered complete when __(name)__ independently completes the task on __(#)__ consecutive trials.

- Without prompting, __(name)__ will independently manage verbal aggression by implementing an exercise routine when agitated, __(# of trials)__ per __(day)__. This is a training objective that will be considered complete when __(name)__ independently completes the skill on __(#)__ consecutive trials.

TRAINING OBJECTIVES TO IMPROVE STRESS MANAGEMENT SKILLS

- Without prompting, ___(name)___ will independently manage verbal aggression by seeking out peers or staff to talk to when agitated, _(# of trials)_ per (day). This is a training objective that will be considered complete when __(name)__ independently completes the skill on __(#)__ consecutive trials.

- Without prompting, ___(name)___ will independently manage self-abusive behavior by removing self from stressful stimuli when agitated, _(# of trials)_ per (day). This is a training objective that will be considered complete when __(name)__ independently completes the skill on __(#)__ consecutive trials.

- Without prompting, ___(name)___ will independently manage self-abusive behavior by implementing deep breathing techniques when agitated, _(# of trials)_ per (day). This is a training objective that will be considered complete when __(name)__ independently completes the task on __(#)__ consecutive trials.

- Without prompting, ___(name)___ will independently manage self-abusive behavior by implementing positive self-talk and imagery when agitated, _(# of trials)_ per (day). This is a training objective that will be considered complete when __(name)__ independently completes the task on __(#)__ consecutive trials.

- Without prompting, ___(name)___ will independently manage self-abusive behavior by implementing an exercise routine when agitated, _(# of trials)_ per (day). This is a training objective that will be considered complete when __(name)__ independently completes the skill on __(#)__ consecutive trials.

- Without prompting, ___(name)___ will independently manage self-abusive behavior by seeking out peers and staff to talk to when agitated, _(# of trials)_ per (day). This is a training objective that will be considered complete when __(name)__ independently completes the skill on __(#)__ consecutive trials.

- Without prompting, ___(name)___ will independently manage sexual behavior by restraining from inappropriate displays of affection, _(# of trials)_ per (day). This is a training objective that will be considered complete when __(name)__ independently completes the skill on __(#)__ consecutive trials.

- Without prompting, ___(name)___ will independently manage destructive behavior by refraining from destroying property, _(# of trials)_ per (day). This is a training objective that will be considered complete when __(name)__ independently completes the task on __(#)__ consecutive trials.

- Without prompting, ___(name)___ will independently respect the property of others by refraining from taking property that belongs to someone else, _(# of trials)_ per (day). This is a training objective that will be considered complete when __(name)__ independently completes the skill on __(#)__ consecutive trials.

TRAINING OBJECTIVES TO IMPROVE STRESS MANAGEMENT SKILLS

- Without prompting, __(name)__ will independently weigh consequences of actions before making decisions, _(# of trials)_ per (day). This is a training objective that will be considered complete when _(name)_ independently completes the skill on ___(#)_ _ consecutive trials.

- Without prompting, _(name)_ will manage repetitive behavior by demonstrating self-control, _(# of trials)_ per (day). This is a training objective that will be considered complete when _(name)_ independently completes the skill on ___(#)__ consecutive trials.

- Without prompting, __(name)__ will manage repetitive behavior by refraining from excessive preoccupation with objects, _(# of trials)_ per (day). This is a training objective that will be considered complete when _(name)_ independently completes the skill on ___(#)__ consecutive trials.

- Without prompting, _(name)_ will independently remain focused on a specific activity for extended periods of time, _(# of trials)_ per (day). This is a training objective that will be considered complete when _(name)_ independently completes the skill on ___(#)__ consecutive trials.

- Without prompting, ___(name)___ will independently remain focused on a specific activity with others for an allotted amount of time, _(# of trials)_ per (day). This is a training objective that will be considered complete when _(name)_ independently completes the skill on ___(#)__ consecutive trials.

- Without prompting, __(name)__ will independently refrain from dangerous behaviors by refraining from eating or putting non-edible items in mouth, _(# of trials)_ per (day). This is a training objective that will be considered complete when __(name)__ independently completes the skill on ___(#)__ consecutive trials.

- Without prompting, ___(name)___ will independently refrain from hording behaviors and inappropriate amounts of food and/or objects, _(# of trials)_ per (day). This is a training objective that will be considered complete when _(name)_ independently completes the skill on ___(#)__ consecutive trials.

PERSONAL AWARENESS

Assistance Objectives (To Maintain Skills)

&

Training Objectives (To Gain and Improve Upon Skills)

Browse a few innovative ideas.....

ASSISTANCE OBJECTIVES TO MAINTAIN PERSONAL AWARENESS SKILLS

- With assistance, __(name)__ will practice monitoring self through anger/stress management techniques __(# of trials)__ per _(day/week/or month)_. This is an assistance objective that will focus on participation in the skill area so that to maintain level of functioning. The objective will cease when __(name)__ no longer is interested or feels staff assistance necessary.

- With assistance, __(name)__ will participate in a group self-advocacy meeting _(# of trials)_ times per _(day/week/or month)_. This is an assistance objective that will focus on participation in the skill area so that to maintain level of functioning. The objective will cease when __(name)__ no longer is interested or feels staff assistance necessary.

- With assistance, __(name)__ will participate in a group level of satisfaction meeting, _(# of trials)_ per _____(day/week/or month)_. This is an assistance objective that will focus on participation in the skill area so that to maintain level of functioning. The objective will cease when __(name)__ no longer is interested or feels staff assistance necessary.

- With assistance, __(name)__ will review personal information such as address and phone number, _(# of trials)_ times per _(day/week/or month)_. This is an assistance objective that will focus on participation in the skill area so that to maintain level of functioning. The objective will cease when __(name)__ no longer is interested or feels staff assistance necessary.

- With assistance, __(name)__ will explore self-interests by participating in community volunteer experiences of choice, _(# of trials)_ times per _(day/week/or month)_. This is an assistance objective that will focus on participation in the skill area so that to maintain level of functioning. The objective will cease when __(name)__ no longer is interested or feels staff assistance necessary.

- With assistance, __(name)__ will practice personal awareness skills by keeping an anger diary, _(# of trials)_ times per _(day/week/or month)_. This is an assistance objective that will focus on participation in the skill area so that to maintain level of functioning. The objective will cease when __(name)__ no longer is interested or feels staff assistance necessary.

- With assistance, __(name)__ will practice personal awareness skills by identifying and listing current life stressors, _(# of trials)_ times per _(day/week/or month)_. This is an assistance objective that will focus on participation in the skill area so that to maintain level of functioning. The objective will cease when __(name)__ no longer is interested or feels staff assistance necessary.

ASSISTANCE OBJECTIVES TO MAINTAIN PERSONAL AWARENESS SKILLS

- With assistance, __(name)__ will practice utilizing the library to explore topics and hobbies of interest, _(# of trials)_ times per (day/week/or month). This is an assistance objective that will focus on participation in the skill area so that to maintain level of functioning. The objective will cease when __(name)__ no longer is interested or feels staff assistance necessary.

- With assistance, __(name)__ will practice personal awareness skills by creating a daily schedule of priorities, _(# of trials)_ times per (day/week/or month). This is an assistance objective that will focus on participation in the skill area so that to maintain level of functioning. The objective will cease when __(name)__ no longer is interested or feels staff assistance necessary.

- With assistance, __(name)__ will engage in creative writing activities that promote personal awareness by listing five personal qualities he/she likes and five personal qualities he/she dislikes, _(# of trials)_ times per (day/week/or month). This is an assistance objective that will focus on participation in the skill area so that to maintain level of functioning. The objective will cease when __(name)__ no longer is interested or feels staff assistance necessary.

- With assistance, __(name)__ will engage in self-exploration by identifying personal goals for the upcoming (day/week/or month). This is an assistance objective that will focus on participation in the skill area so that to maintain level of functioning. The objective will cease when __(name)__ no longer is interested or feels staff assistance necessary.

- With assistance, __(name)__ will engage in personal awareness through art by identifying feelings on paper, _(# of trials)_ times per (day/week/or month). This is an assistance objective that will focus on participation in the skill area so that to maintain level of functioning. The objective will cease when __(name)__ no longer is interested or feels staff assistance necessary.

- With assistance, __(name)__ will explore reading materials and information related to hobbies/topics of interest, _(# of trials)_ times per (day/week/or month). This is an assistance objective that will focus on participation in the skill area so that to maintain level of functioning. The objective will cease when __(name)__ no longer is interested or feels staff assistance necessary.

- With assistance, __(name)__ will explore music that promotes personal awareness and expression, _(# of trials)_ times per (day/week/or month). This is an assistance objective that will focus on participation in the skill area so that to maintain level of functioning. The objective will cease when __(name)__ no longer is interested or feels staff assistance necessary.

ASSISTANCE OBJECTIVES TO MAINTAIN PERSONAL AWARENESS SKILLS

- With assistance,__(name)__ will explore community groups and organizations that promote personal awareness, _(# of trials)_ times per _(day/week/or month)_. This is an assistance objective that will focus on participation in the skill area so that to maintain level of functioning. The objective will cease when __(name)__ no longer is interested or feels staff assistance necessary.

- With assistance, __(name)__ will practice personal awareness skills by speaking at appropriate tones and refraining form talking over others when getting to know peers, _(# of trials)_ times per _(day/week/or month)_. This is an assistance objective that will focus on participation in the skill area so that to maintain level of functioning. The objective will cease when __(name)__ no longer is interested or feels staff assistance necessary.

- With assistance, __(name)__ will practice the use of awareness skills through the use of personal boundaries while interacting with others, _(# of trials)_ times per _(day/ week/or month)_. This is an assistance objective that will focus on participation in the skill area so that to maintain level of functioning. The objective will cease when _(name)_ no longer is interested or feels staff assistance necessary.

Browse a few innovative ideas…..

TRAINING OBJECTIVES TO IMPROVE PERSONAL AWARENESS SKILLS

- Without prompting, _(name)_ will independently state his/her address and telephone number, _(# of trials)_ times per _(day/week/or month)_. This is a training objective that will be considered complete when _(name)_ independently completes the task in a correct fashion on _(#)_ consecutive trials.

- Without prompting, _(name)_ will independently engage in creative writing skills that promote personal awareness by listing five personal qualities he/she likes and five personal qualities he/she dislikes, _(# of trials)_ times per _(day/week/or month)_. This is a training objective that will be considered complete when _(name)_ independently completes the task on _(#)_ consecutive trials.

- Without prompting, _(name)_ will independently engage in personal awareness skills by identifying goals for the upcoming week, month, and or year. This objective will occur _(# of trials)_ times per _(day/week/or month)_. This is a training objective that will be considered complete when _(name)_ independently completes the task on _(#)_ consecutive trials.

- Without prompting, _(name)_ will independently engage in self-exploration through journal writing, _(# of trials)_ times per _(day/week/or month)_. This is a training objective that will be considered complete when _(name)_ independently completes the task on _(#)_ consecutive trials.

- Without assistance, _(name)_ will independently engage in personal awareness by keeping an anger diary, _(# of trials)_ times per _(day/week/or month)_. This is a training objective that will be considered complete when _(name)_ independently completes the task on _(#)_ consecutive trials.

- Without assistance, _(name)_ will engage in personal awareness by identifying and listing current life stressors, _(# of trials)_ times per _(day/week/or month)_. This is a training objective that will be considered complete when _(name)_ independently completes the task on _(#)_ consecutive trials.

- Without assistance, _(name)_ will independently utilize the library to explore topics and hobbies of interest, _(# of trials)_ times per _(day/week/or month)_. This is a training objective that will be considered complete when _(name)_ independently completes the task on _(#)_ consecutive trials.

- Without assistance, _(name)_ will independently engage in self-awareness skills by demonstrating the ability to create a daily schedule of priorities, _(# of trials)_ times per _(day/week/or month)_. This is a training objective that will be considered complete when _(name)_ independently completes the task on _(#)_ consecutive trials.

TRAINING OBJECTIVES TO IMPROVE PERSONAL AWARENESS SKILLS

- Without prompting, __(name)__ will independently implement personal awareness skills by speaking at appropriate tones and refraining form talking over others, _(# of trials)_ times per (day/week/or month). This is a training objective that will be considered complete when __(name)__ independently completes the task on __(#)_ _ consecutive trials.

- Without prompting, __(name)__ will implement appropriate personal awareness skills through the use of personal boundaries while interacting with others, _(# of trials)_ times per (day/week/or month). This is a training objective that will be considered complete when _(name)_ independently completes the task on __(#)_ consecutive trials.

- Without prompting, __(name)__ will implement stress management techniques _(# of trials)_ per (day/week/or month). This is a training objective that will be considered complete when _(name)_ independently completes the task in a correct fashion on __(#)_ consecutive trials.

- Without prompting, __(name)__ will engage in a group "self-advocacy" and/or "satisfaction with services" meeting _(# of trials)_ times per (day/week/or month). This is a training objective that will be considered complete when __(name)_ independently completes the task in a correct fashion on __(#)__ consecutive trials.

- Without prompting, __(name)__ will independently explore personal interests by participating in community volunteer experiences of choice, _(# of trials)_ times per (day/week/or month). This is a training objective that will be considered complete when _(name)_ independently completes the task in a correct fashion on __(#)_ consecutive trials.

- Without assistance, __(name)__ will independently explore reading materials and information related to hobbies/topics of interest, _(# of trials)_ times per (day/week/ or month). This is a training objective that will be considered complete when _(name)_ independently completes the task in a correct fashion on __(#)_ consecutive trials.

- Without assistance, __(name)__ will independently seek out and explore music that promotes personal awareness and expression, _(# of trials)_ times per (day/week/or month). This is a training objective that will be considered complete when __(name)_ independently completes the task on __(#)_ consecutive trials.

- Without assistance, __(name)__ will independently seek out and explore community groups and organizations that promote self-awareness, _(# of trials)_ times per (day/ week/or month). This is a training objective that will be considered complete when (name)_ independently completes the task on __(#)_ consecutive trials.

TIME MANAGEMENT

Assistance Objectives (To Maintain Skills)

&

Training Objectives (To Gain and Improve Upon Skills)

Browse a few innovative ideas.....

ASSISTANCE OBJECTIVES TO MAINTAIN TIME MANAGEMENT SKILLS

- With assistance, __(name)__ will practice stating the correct time to the minute, __(# of trials)__ times per (day/week/or month). This is an assistance objective that will focus on participation in the skill area so that to maintain level of functioning. The objective will cease when __(name)__ no longer is interested or feels staff assistance necessary.

- With assistance, __(name)__ will practice stating the correct time to the quarter hour, __(# of trials)__ times per (day/week/or month). This is an assistance objective that will focus on participation in the skill area so that to maintain level of functioning. The objective will cease when __(name)__ no longer is interested or feels staff assistance necessary.

- With assistance, __(name)__ will practice stating the correct time to the half hour, __(# of trials)__ times per (day/week/or month). This is an assistance objective that will focus on participation in the skill area so that to maintain level of functioning. The objective will cease when __(name)__ no longer is interested or feels staff assistance necessary.

- With assistance, __(name)__ will practice stating the correct time to the hour, __(# of trials)__ times per (day/week/or month). This is an assistance objective that will focus on participation in the skill area so that to maintain level of functioning. The objective will cease when __(name)__ no longer is interested or feels staff assistance necessary.

- With assistance, __(name)__ will practice matching the appropriate activities to time of day to the minute, __(# of trials)__ times per (day/week/or month). This is an assistance objective that will focus on participation in the skill area so that to maintain level of functioning. The objective will cease when __(name)__ no longer is interested or feels staff assistance necessary.

- With assistance, __(name)__ will practice utilizing time management skills by completing his/her morning dressing routine in a timely fashion. This is an assistance objective that will focus on participation in the skill area so that to maintain level of functioning. The objective will cease when __(name)__ no longer is interested or feels staff assistance necessary.

- With assistance, __(name)__ will identify the correct time of day by utilizing his/her wristwatch, __(# of trials)__ times a day. This is an assistance objective that will focus on participation in the skill area so that to maintain level of functioning. The objective will cease when __(name)__ no longer is interested or feels staff assistance necessary.

ASSISTANCE OBJECTIVES TO MAINTAIN TIME MANAGEMENT SKILLS

- With assistance, __(name)__ will utilize time management skills by remaining on a specified task for thirty consecutive minutes without becoming distracted _(# of trials)_ times a day. This is an assistance objective that will focus on participation in the skill area so that to maintain level of functioning. The objective will cease when (name) no longer is interested or feels staff assistance necessary.

- With assistance, __(name)__ will utilize time management skills in order to complete daily assigned chores in an appropriate amount of time, _(# of trials)_ times a day. This is an assistance objective that will focus on participation in the skill area so that to maintain level of functioning. The objective will cease when _(name)_ no longer is interested or feels staff assistance necessary.

- With assistance, __(name)__ will utilize time management skills by correctly identifying the appropriate time for lunch, _(# of trials)_ per (day/week/or month). This is an assistance objective that will focus on participation in the skill area so that to maintain level of functioning. The objective will cease when _(name)_ no longer is interested or feels staff assistance necessary.

- With assistance, _(name)_ will remain on a specific task for fifteen minutes, _(# of trials)_ times per (day/week/or month). This is an assistance objective that will focus on participation in the skill area so that to maintain level of functioning. The objective will cease when _(name)_ no longer is interested or feels staff assistance necessary.

Browse a few innovative ideas.....

TRAINING OBJECTIVES TO IMPROVE TIME MANAGEMENT SKILLS

- Without prompting, __(name)__ will independently state the correct time to the minute, _(# of trials)_ times per (day/week/or month). This is a training objective that will be considered complete when __(name)__ independently, without prompting, completes the task on for the set amount of time for __(#)__ consecutive trials.

- Without prompting, __(name)__ will independently state the correct time to the quarter hour, _(# of trials)_ times per (day/week/or month). This is a training objective that will be considered complete when __(name)__ independently, without prompting, completes the task on for the set amount of time for __(#)__ consecutive trials.

- Without prompting, __(name)__ will independently state the correct time to the half hour, _(# of trials)_ times per (day/week/or month). This is a training objective that will be considered complete when __(name)__ independently, without prompting, completes the task on for the set amount of time for __(#)__ consecutive trials.

- Without prompting, __(name)__ will independently state the correct time to the hour, _(# of trials)_ times per (day/week/or month). This is a training objective that will be considered complete when __(name)__ independently, without prompting, completes the task on for the set amount of time for __(#)__ consecutive trials.

- Without prompting, __(name)__ will independently match the appropriate activities to time of day to the minute, _(# of trials)_ times per (day/week/or month). This is a training objective that will be considered complete when __(name)__ independently, without prompting, completes the task on for the set amount of time for __(#)__ consecutive trials.

- Without prompting, __(name)__ will independently utilize time management skills by completing his/her morning dressing routine in a timely fashion, _(# of trials)_ times per day. This is a training objective considered complete when __(name)__ uses appropriate time management skills during morning preparation on __(#)__ consecutive trials.

- Without prompting, __(name)__ will independently identify the correct time of day by utilizing his/her wristwatch, _(# of trials)_ times a day. This is a training objective that will be considered complete when __(name)__ independently identifies the correct time of day on __(#)__ consecutive trials.

- Without assistance, __(name)__ will independently utilize time management skills by remaining on a specified task for thirty consecutive minutes without becoming distracted, _(# of trials)_ times a day. The objective will be considered complete when __(name)__ has independently remained on task, without prompting, for __(#)__ _ consecutive trials.

TRAINING OBJECTIVES TO IMPROVE TIME MANAGEMENT SKILLS

- Without prompting, __(name)__ will independently utilize time management skills in order to complete daily assigned chores in an appropriate amount of time, _(# of trials)_ times a day. This is a training objective that will be considered complete when __(name)__ independently, without prompting, completes the task on __(#)__ consecutive trials.

- Without prompting, __(name)__ will independently utilize time management skills by correctly identifying the appropriate time for lunch, _(# of trials)_ per (day/week/ or month). The training objective will be considered complete when __(name)__ has correctly completed the task independently, without prompting, on __(#)__ consecutive trials.

- Without prompting, __(name)__ will independently remain on a specific task for fifteen minutes, _(# of trials)_ times per (day/week/or month). This is a training objective that will be considered complete when __(name)__ independently, without prompting, completes the task on for the set amount of time for __(#)__ consecutive trials.

LEARNING & PROBLEM SOLVING

Assistance Objectives (To Maintain Skills)

&

Training Objectives (To Gain and Improve Upon Skills)

Browse a few innovative ideas.....

ASSISTANCE OBJECTIVES TO MAINTAIN LEARNING AND PROBLEM SOLVING SKILLS

- With assistance, __(name)__ will practice verbally stating the value of coin and bill denominations, _(# of trials)_ times per (day/week/or month). This is an assistance objective that will focus on participation in the skill area so that to maintain level of functioning. The objective will cease when __(name)__ no longer is interested or feels staff assistance necessary.

- With assistance, __(name)__ will practice identifying coinage and paper currency, _(# of trials)_ times per (day/week/or month). This is an assistance objective that will focus on participation in the skill area so that to maintain level of functioning. The objective will cease when __(name)__ no longer is interested or feels staff assistance necessary.

- With prompting, __(name)__ will practice remaining on a specific task for 15 minutes, _(# of trials)_ times per (day/week/or month). This is an assistance objective that will focus on participation in the skill area so that to maintain level of functioning. The objective will cease when __(name)__ no longer is interested or feels staff assistance necessary.

- With assistance, __(name)__ will practice holding a pencil in the proper position for writing, _(# of trials)_ times per (day/week/or month). This is an assistance objective that will focus on participation in the skill area so that to maintain level of functioning. The objective will cease when __(name)__ no longer is interested or feels staff assistance necessary.

- With assistance, __(name)__ will practice identifying simple sight words, _(# of trials)_ times per (day/week/or month). This is an assistance objective that will focus on participation in the skill area so that to maintain level of functioning. The objective will cease when __(name)__ no longer is interested or feels staff assistance necessary.

- With assistance, __(name)__ will practice sorting and matching coins, _(# of trials)_ times per (day/week/or month). This is an assistance objective that will focus on participation in the skill area so that to maintain level of functioning. The objective will cease when __(name)__ no longer is interested or feels staff assistance necessary.

- With assistance, __(name)__ will practice managing a checking account in an independent fashion, _(# of trials)_ times per (day/week/or month). This is an assistance objective that will focus on participation in the skill area so that to maintain level of functioning. The objective will cease when __(name)__ no longer is interested or feels staff assistance necessary.

ASSISTANCE OBJECTIVES TO MAINTAIN LEARNING AND PROBLEM SOLVING SKILLS

- With assistance, __(name)__ will practice writing and singing personal checks, __(# of trials)__ times per __(day/week/or month)__. This is an assistance objective that will focus on participation in the skill area so that to maintain level of functioning. The objective will cease when __(name)__ no longer is interested or feels staff assistance necessary.

- With assistance, __(name)__ will practice shopping comparatively for groceries, __(# of trials)__ times per __(day/week/or month)__. This is an assistance objective that will focus on participation in the skill area so that to maintain level of functioning. The objective will cease when __(name)__ no longer is interested or feels staff assistance necessary.

- With assistance, __(name)__ will practice budgeting personal expenses, __(# of trials)__ times per __(day/week/or month)__. This is an assistance objective that will focus on participation in the skill area so that to maintain level of functioning. The objective will cease when __(name)__ no longer is interested or feels staff assistance necessary.

- With assistance, __(name)__ will practice adding prices of two to three items, __(# of trials)__ times per __(day/week/or month)__. This is an assistance objective that will focus on participation in the skill area so that to maintain level of functioning. The objective will cease when __(name)__ no longer is interested or feels staff assistance necessary.

- With assistance, __(name)__ will practice adding items on a calculator, __(# of trials)__ times per __(day/week/or month)__. This is an assistance objective that will focus on participation in the skill area so that to maintain level of functioning. The objective will cease when __(name)__ no longer is interested or feels staff assistance necessary.

- With assistance, __(name)__ will practice writing dollars and cents in decimal notation, __(# of trials)__ times per __(day/week/or month)__. This is an assistance objective that will focus on participation in the skill area so that to maintain level of functioning. The objective will cease when __(name)__ no longer is interested or feels staff assistance necessary.

- With assistance, __(name)__ will practice reading dollars and cents in decimal notation, __(# of trials)__ times per __(day/week/or month)__. This is an assistance objective that will focus on participation in the skill area so that to maintain level of functioning. The objective will cease when __(name)__ no longer is interested or feels staff assistance necessary.

- With assistance, __(name)__ will practice counting various coin and bill combinations in a correct fashion, __(# of trials)__ times per __(day/week/or month)__. This is an assistance objective that will focus on participation in the skill area so that to maintain level of functioning. The objective will cease when __(name)__ no longer is interested or feels staff assistance necessary.

ASSISTANCE OBJECTIVES TO MAINTAIN LEARNING AND PROBLEM SOLVING SKILLS

- With assistance, __(name)__ will practice identifying bill denominations, __(# of trials)__ times per __(day/week/or month)__. This is an assistance objective that will focus on participation in the skill area so that to maintain level of functioning. The objective will cease when __(name)__ no longer is interested or feels staff assistance necessary.

- With assistance, __(name)__ will practice counting coin combinations up to $1.00, __(# of trials)__ times per __(day/week/or month)__. This is an assistance objective that will focus on participation in the skill area so that to maintain level of functioning. The objective will cease when __(name)__ no longer is interested or feels staff assistance necessary.

- With assistance, __(name)__ will practice stating the value of each coin, __(# of trials)__ times per __(day/week/or month)__. This is an assistance objective that will focus on participation in the skill area so that to maintain level of functioning. The objective will cease when __(name)__ no longer is interested or feels staff assistance necessary.

- With assistance, __(name)__ will practice identifying coins by name, __(# of trials)__ times per __(day/week/or month)__. This is an assistance objective that will focus on participation in the skill area so that to maintain level of functioning. The objective will cease when __(name)__ no longer is interested or feels staff assistance necessary.

- With assistance, __(name)__ will practice the understanding of more and less when utilizing money, __(# of trials)__ times per __(day/week/or month)__. This is an assistance objective that will focus on participation in the skill area so that to maintain level of functioning. The objective will cease when __(name)__ no longer is interested or feels staff assistance necessary.

- With assistance, __(name)__ will practice counting objects (one to ten), __(# of trials)__ times per __(day/week/or month)__. This is an assistance objective that will focus on participation in the skill area so that to maintain level of functioning. The objective will cease when __(name)__ no longer is interested or feels staff assistance necessary.

- With assistance, __(name)__ will practice recognizing numbers, __(# of trials)__ times per __(day/week/or month)__. This is an assistance objective that will focus on participation in the skill area so that to maintain level of functioning. The objective will cease when __(name)__ no longer is interested or feels staff assistance necessary.

- With assistance, __(name)__ will practice identifying appropriate tools/utensils for a specific task, __(# of trials)__ times per __(day/week/or month)__. This is an assistance objective that will focus on participation in the skill area so that to maintain level of functioning. The objective will cease when __(name)__ no longer is interested or feels staff assistance necessary.

Browse a few innovative ideas.....

TRAINING OBJECTIVES TO IMPROVE LEARNING AND PROBLEM SOLVING SKILLS

- Without assistance, __(name)__ will verbally state the value of coin and bill denominations, _(# of trials)_ times per (day/week/or month). The criteria for this training objective will be considered met when the task has been completed correctly in an independent fashion, without prompting, on _(#)_ consecutive trials.

- Without prompting, _(name)_ will independently identify coinage and paper currency with 100% accuracy, _(# of trials)_ times per (day/week/or month). This is a training objective that will be considered complete when __(name)__ independently identifies the correct amount on _(#)_ consecutive trials.

- Without prompting, __(name)__ will independently remain on a specific task for 15 minutes, _(# of trials)_ times per (day/week/or month). This is a training objective that will be considered complete when _(name)__ independently addresses the task on _(#)_ consecutive trials.

- Without prompting, __(name)__ will independently hold a pencil in the proper position for writing, _(# of trials)_ times per (day/week/or month). This is a training objective that will be considered complete when __(name)__ independently addresses the task in a correct fashion on _(#)_ consecutive trials.

- Without assistance, __(name)__ will independently identify simple sight words, _(# of trials)_ times per (day/week/or month). This is a training objective that will be considered complete when __(name)__ independently addresses the task in a correct fashion on _(#)_ consecutive trials.

- Without assistance, __(name)__ will correctly sort and match coins independently, _(# of trials)_ times per (day/week/or month). The criteria for this training objective will be considered met when the task has been completed correctly in an independent fashion, without prompting, on _(#)_ consecutive trials.

- Without assistance, __(name)__ will correctly manager a checking account in an independent fashion, _(# of trials)_ times per (day/week/or month). The criteria for this training objective will be considered met when the task has been completed correctly in an independent fashion, without prompting, on _(#)_ consecutive trials.

- Without assistance, __(name)__ will independently write checks in a correct fashion, _ (# of trials)_ times per (day/week/or month). The criteria for this training objective will be considered met when the task has been completed correctly in an independent fashion, without prompting, on _(#)_ consecutive trials.

- Without assistance, __(name)__ will independently shop comparatively for groceries, _(# of trials)_ times per (day/week/or month). The criteria for this training objective will be considered met when the task has been completed correctly in an independent fashion, without prompting, on _(#)_ consecutive trials.

TRAINING OBJECTIVES TO IMPROVE LEARNING AND PROBLEM SOLVING SKILLS

- Without assistance, ___(name)___ will independently budget expenses in a correct fashion, _(# of trials)_ times per (day/week/or month). The criteria for this training objective will be considered met when the task has been completed correctly in an independent fashion, without prompting, on (#) consecutive trials.

- Without assistance, ___(name)___ will independently add prices of three items in a correct fashion, _(# of trials)_ times per (day/week/or month). The criteria for this training objective will be considered met when the task has been completed correctly in an independent fashion, without prompting, on (#) consecutive trials.

- Without assistance, ___(name)___ will independently add items on a calculator, _(# of trials)_ times per (day/week/or month). The criteria for this training objective will be considered met when the task has been completed correctly in an independent fashion, without prompting, on (#) consecutive trials.

- Without assistance, ___(name)___ will independently write dollars and cents in decimal notation, _(# of trials)_ times per (day/week/or month). The criteria for this training objective will be considered met when the task has been completed correctly in an independent fashion, without prompting, on (#) consecutive trials.

- Without assistance, ___(name)___ will independently read dollars and cents in decimal notation, _(# of trials)_ times per (day/week/or month). The criteria for this training objective will be considered met when the task has been completed correctly in an independent fashion, without prompting, on (#) consecutive trials.

- Without assistance, ___(name)___ will independently count various coin and bill combinations in a correct fashion, _(# of trials)_ times per (day/week/or month). The criteria for this training objective will be considered met when the task has been completed correctly in an independent fashion, without prompting, on (#) consecutive trials.

- Without assistance, ___(name)___ will independently identify bill denominations, _(# of trials)_ times per (day/week/or month). The criteria for this training objective will be considered met when the task has been completed correctly in an independent fashion, without prompting, on (#) consecutive trials.

- Without assistance, ___(name)___ will independently count coin combinations up to $1.00, _(# of trials)_ times per (day/week/or month). The criteria for this training objective will be considered met when the task has been completed correctly in an independent fashion, without prompting, on (#) consecutive trials.

- Without assistance, ___(name)___ will independently state the value of each coin, _(# of trials)_ times per (day/week/or month). The criteria for this training objective will be considered met when the task has been completed correctly in an independent fashion, without prompting, on (#) consecutive trials.

TRAINING OBJECTIVES TO IMPROVE LEARNING AND PROBLEM SOLVING SKILLS

- Without assistance, ___(name)___ will independently identify coins by name, _(# of trials)_ times per (day/week/or month). The criteria for this training objective will be considered met when the task has been completed correctly in an independent fashion, without prompting, on _(#)_ consecutive trials.

- Without assistance, ___(name)___ will independently demonstrate the understanding of more and less when utilizing money, _(# of trials)_ times per (day/week/or month). The criteria for this training objective will be considered met when the task has been completed correctly in an independent fashion, without prompting, on _(#)_ consecutive trials.

- Without assistance, ___(name)___ will independently count objects (one to ten), _(# of trials)_ times per (day/week/or month). The criteria for this training objective will be considered met when the task has been completed correctly in an independent fashion, without prompting, on _(#)_ consecutive trials.

- Without assistance, ___(name)___ will independently recognize numbers, _(# of trials)_ times per (day/week/or month). The criteria for this training objective will be considered met when the task has been completed correctly in an independent fashion, without prompting, on _(#)_ consecutive trials.

- Without assistance, ___(name)___ will independently identify appropriate tool/utensil for a specific task, _(# of trials)_ times per (day/week/or month). The criteria for this training objective will be considered met when the task has been completed correctly in an independent fashion, without prompting, on _(#)_ consecutive trials.

ACCESSING COMMUNITY RESOURCES

Assistance Objectives (To Maintain Skills)

&

Training Objectives (To Gain and Improve Upon Skills)

ASSISTANCE OBJECTIVES TO MAINTAIN COMMUNITY RESOURCE SKILLS

- With staff assistance, __(name)__ will review local newspapers and magazines to determine current events and activities of interest, _(# of trials)_ times per (day/ week/or month). This is an assistance objective that will focus on participation in the skill area so that to maintain level of functioning. The objective will cease when (name) no longer is interested or feels staff assistance necessary.

- With assistance, __(name)__ will dine at a selected restaurant of choice _(# of trials)_ times per (day/week/or month). This is an assistance objective that will focus on participation in the skill area so that to maintain level of functioning. The objective will cease when _(name)__ no longer is interested or feels staff assistance necessary.

- With staff assistance, __(name)__ will become familiar with banking methods _(# of trials)_ times per (day/week/or month). This is an assistance objective that will focus on participation in the skill area so that to maintain level of functioning. The objective will cease when _(name)__ no longer is interested or feels staff assistance necessary.

- With assistance, __(name)__ will access the library to check out books of interests, _(# of trials)_ times per (day/week/or month). This is an assistance objective that will focus on participation in the skill area so that to maintain level of functioning. The objective will cease when _(name)__ no longer is interested or feels staff assistance necessary.

- With staff assistance, _(name)_ will contact friends to participate in mutual enjoyable activities, _(# of trials)_ times per (day/week/or month). This is an assistance objective that will focus on participation in the skill area so that to maintain level of functioning. The objective will cease when __(name)__ no longer is interested or feels staff assistance necessary.

- With assistance, __(name)__ will access information using the Internet _(# of trials)_ times per (day/week/or month). This is an assistance objective that will focus on participation in the skill area so that to maintain level of functioning. The objective will cease when _(name)__ no longer is interested or feels staff assistance necessary.

- With assistance, __(name)__ will participate in community volunteer experiences of choice, _(# of trials)_ times per (day/week/or month). This is an assistance objective that will focus on participation in the skill area so that to maintain level of functioning. The objective will cease when __(name)__ no longer is interested or feels staff assistance necessary.

ASSISTANCE OBJECTIVES TO MAINTAIN COMMUNITY RESOURCE SKILLS

- With assistance, __(name)__ will develop an activity calendar, __(# of trials)__ times per (day/week/or month). This is an assistance objective that will focus on participation in the skill area so that to maintain level of functioning. The objective will cease when __(name)__ no longer is interested or feels staff assistance necessary.

- With assistance, (name) will seek out handrails, ramps, and elevators to utilize while maneuvering in the community, _(# of trials)_ times per (day/week/or month). This is an assistance objective that will focus on participation in the skill area so that to maintain level of functioning. The objective will cease when (name) no longer is interested or feels staff assistance necessary.

- With assistance, __(name)__ will practice presenting I.D./Medical Info. card upon request, (# of trials) times per day. This is an assistance objective that will focus on participation in the skill area so that to maintain level of functioning. The objective will cease when __(name)__ no longer is interested or feels staff assistance necessary.

- With assistance, __(name)__ will practice locating numbers of interest in the telephone directory, (# of trials) times per (day/week/or month). This is an assistance objective that will focus on participation in the skill area so that to maintain level of functioning. The objective will cease when __(name)__ no longer is interested or feels staff assistance necessary.

- With assistance, __(name)__ will practice locating the address of merchants of interest in the blue and yellow pages of the telephone directory, (# of trials) times per (day/ week/or month). This is an assistance objective that will focus on participation in the skill area so that to maintain level of functioning. The objective will cease when (name) no longer is interested or feels staff assistance necessary.

- With assistance, __(name)__ will practice dialing numbers of interest presented orally by staff, (# of trials) times per (day/week/or month). This is an assistance objective that will focus on participation in the skill area so that to maintain level of functioning. The objective will cease when __(name)__ no longer is interested or feels staff assistance necessary.

- With assistance, __(name)__ will practice dialing written numbers of interest, (# of trials) times per (day/week/or month). This is an assistance objective that will focus on participation in the skill area so that to maintain level of functioning. The objective will cease when __(name)__ no longer is interested or feels staff assistance necessary.

- With assistance, __(name)__ will make a purchase utilizing a vending machine, (# of trials) times per (day/week/or month). This is an assistance objective that will focus on participation in the skill area so that to maintain level of functioning. The objective will cease when __(name)__ no longer is interested or feels staff assistance necessary.

ASSISTANCE OBJECTIVES TO MAINTAIN COMMUNITY RESOURCE SKILLS

- With assistance, __(name)__ will select and order items for purchase in the community, (# of trials) times per (day/week/or month). This is an assistance objective that will focus on participation in the skill area so that to maintain level of functioning. The objective will cease when __(name)__ no longer is interested or feels staff assistance necessary.

- With assistance, __(name)__ will order a meal at a restaurant of choice, (# of trials) times per (day/week/or month). This is an assistance objective that will focus on participation in the skill area so that to maintain level of functioning. The objective will cease when __(name)__ no longer is interested or feels staff assistance necessary.

- With assistance, __(name)__ will practice paying bus/taxi fare, (# of trials) times per (day/week/or month). This is an assistance objective that will focus on participation in the skill area so that to maintain level of functioning. The objective will cease when __(name)__ no longer is interested or feels staff assistance necessary.

- With assistance, __(name)__ will practice recognizing and getting off at the correct stop when utilizing the bus/taxi, (# of trials) times per (day/week/or month). This is an assistance objective that will focus on participation in the skill area so that to maintain level of functioning. The objective will cease when __(name)__ no longer is interested or feels staff assistance necessary.

- With assistance, __(name)__ will practice reading a bus schedule, (# of trials) times per (day/week/or month). This is an assistance objective that will focus on participation in the skill area so that to maintain level of functioning. The objective will cease when __(name)__ no longer is interested or feels staff assistance necessary.

- With assistance, __(name)__ will practice identifying community signs, (# of trials) times per (day/week/or month). This is an assistance objective that will focus on participation in the skill area so that to maintain level of functioning. The objective will cease when __(name)__ no longer is interested or feels staff assistance necessary.

- With assistance, __(name)__ will practice stopping at curbs/street intersections, (# of trials) times per (day/week/or month). This is an assistance objective that will focus on participation in the skill area so that to maintain level of functioning. The objective will cease when __(name)__ no longer is interested or feels staff assistance necessary.

- With assistance, __(name)__ will practice identifying community safety/survival signs, (# of trials) times per (day/week/or month). This is an assistance objective that will focus on participation in the skill area so that to maintain level of functioning. The objective will cease when __(name)__ no longer is interested or feels staff assistance necessary.

Browse a few innovative ideas…..

TRAINING OBJECTIVES TO IMPROVE COMMUNITY RESOURCE SKILLS

- Without prompting, __(name)__ will independently seek out community events and recreational activities of interest _(# of trials)_ times per (day/week/or month). This is a training objectives designed to improve community resource skills. The objective will be considered complete when __(name)__ completes the task independently on __(#)__ consecutive trials.

- Without prompting , __(name)__ will independently participate in a planned community outing of choice _(# of trials)_ times per (day/week/or month). This is a training objective designed to improve community access and utilization skills. This objective will be met when the task is completed independently on __(#)__ consecutive trials.

- Without assistance, __(name)__ will independently make a simple purchase in the community _(# of trials)_ times per (day/week/or month). This is a training objective that is designed so that community access and utilization skills are improved. The objective will be considered complete when the task has been completed independently on __(#)__ consecutive trials.

- Without prompting, __(name)__ will independently utilize the crosswalk by stopping and abiding traffic signals before crossing the street _(# of trials)_ times a (day/week/or month). This is a training objective that will be considered complete when (name) independently performs the task on __(#)__ consecutive trials.

- Without assistance, __(name)__ will independently implement the correct technological functions to access the Internet, _(# of trials)_ times a (day/week/or month). This is a training objective that is designed to improve independence with this particular skill. This training objective will be considered complete when the task has been performed independently, without prompting, on __(#)__ consecutive trials.

- Without prompting, __(name)__ will seek out handrails, ramps, and elevators to utilize while maneuvering in the community, _(# of trials)_ times per (day/week/or month). This is a training objective that is designed to improve independence with this particular skill. This is a training objective that will be considered complete when the task has been performed independently, without prompting, on __(#)__ consecutive trials.

- Upon request, __(name)__ will independently present I.D./Medical Info. card, _(# of trials)_ times per (day/week/or month). This is a training objective that is designed to improve independence with this particular skill. This is a training objective that will be considered complete when the task has been performed independently, without prompting, on __(#)__ consecutive trials.

TRAINING OBJECTIVES TO IMPROVE COMMUNITY RESOURCE SKILLS

- Without assistance, __(name)__ will independently locate numbers in the telephone directory, _(# of trials)_ times per (day/week/or month). This is a training objective that is designed to improve independence with this particular skill. This is a training objective that will be considered complete when the task has been performed independently, without prompting, on __(#)__ consecutive trials.

- Without assistance, __(name)__ will independently locate the address of merchants in the blue and yellow pages of the telephone directory, _(# of trials)_ times per (day/week/or month). This is a training objective that is designed to improve independence with this particular skill. This is a training objective that will be considered complete when the task has been performed independently, without prompting, on __(#)__ consecutive trials.

- Without assistance, __(name)__ will independently dial numbers of interest presented orally by staff, _(# of trials)_ times per (day/week/or month). This is a training objective that is designed to improve independence with this particular skill. This is a training objective that will be considered complete when the task has been performed independently, without prompting, on __(#)__ consecutive trials.

- Without assistance, __(name)__ will independently dial written numbers of interest, _(# of trials)_ times per (day/week/or month). This is a training objective that is designed to improve independence with this particular skill. This is a training objective that will be considered complete when the task has been performed independently, without prompting, on __(#)__ consecutive trials.

- Without assistance, __(name)__ will independently make a purchase utilizing a vending machine, _(# of trials)_ times per (day/week/or month). This is a training objective that is designed to improve independence with this particular skill. This is a training objective that will be considered complete when the task has been performed independently, without prompting, on __(#)__ consecutive trials.

- Without assistance, __(name)__ will independently select and order items for purchase in the community, _(# of trials)_ times per (day/week/or month). This is a training objective that is designed to improve independence with this particular skill. This is a training objective that will be considered complete when the task has been performed independently, without prompting, on __(#)__ consecutive trials.

- Without assistance, __(name)__ will independently order a meal at a restaurant of choice, _(# of trials)_ times per (day/week/or month). This is a training objective that is designed to improve independence with this particular skill. This is a training objective that will be considered complete when the task has been performed independently, without prompting, on __(#)__ consecutive trials.

TRAINING OBJECTIVES TO IMPROVE COMMUNITY RESOURCE SKILLS

- Without assistance, __(name)__ will demonstrate through role-play the correct manner in which to independently pay bus/taxi fare, __(# of trials)__ times per (day/week/or month). This is a training objective that is designed to improve independence with this particular skill. This is a training objective that will be considered complete when the task has been performed independently, without prompting, on __(#)__ consecutive trials.

- Without assistance, __(name)__ will independently recognize and get off at the correct stop when utilizing the bus/taxi, __(# of trials)__ times per (day/week/or month). This is a training objective that is designed to improve independence with this particular skill. This is a training objective that will be considered complete when the task has been performed independently, without prompting, on __(#)__ consecutive trials.

- Without assistance, __(name)__ will independently read a bus schedule and state the schedule's contents, __(# of trials)__ times per (day/week/or month). This is a training objective that is designed to improve independence with this particular skill. This is a training objective that will be considered complete when the task has been performed independently, without prompting, on __(#)__ consecutive trials.

- Without assistance, __(name)__ will independently identify and state the correct meaning of community signs, __(# of trials)__ times per (day/week/or month). This is a training objective that is designed to improve independence with this particular skill. This is a training objective that will be considered complete when the task has been performed independently, without prompting, on __(#)__ consecutive trials.

- Without assistance, __(name)__ will independently stop at curbs/street intersections, __(# of trials)__ times per (day/week/or month). This is a training objective that is designed to improve independence with this particular skill. This is a training objective that will be considered complete when the task has been performed independently, without prompting, on __(#)__ consecutive trials.

- Without assistance, __(name)__ will independently identify the correct meaning of community safety and survival signs, __(# of trials)__ times per (day/week/or month). This is a training objective that is designed to improve independence with this particular skill. This is a training objective that will be considered complete when the task has been performed independently, without prompting, on __(#)__ consecutive trials.

SECTION THREE

Expanding Options

RESOURCES FOR SPECIAL POPULATIONS

Special Olympics
1325 G Street, NW Suite 500
Washington, DC 20005
(202) 628-3630
http://www.specialolympics.org

The Arc of the United States
The Arc of the United States
1010 Wayne Avenue, Suite 650
Silver Spring, MD 20910
(301) 565-3842
http://thearc.org

Best Buddies International
Best Buddies International
100 SE Second Street, #1990
Miami, FL 33131
(305) 374-2233
http://www.bestbuddies.org

AAMR
444 North Capitol Street, NW Suite 846
Washington, D.C. 20001-1512
(800) 424-3688
 http://www.aamr.org/

American Therapeutic Recreation Association
American Therapeutic Recreation Association
1414 Prince Street, Suite 204
Alexandria, Virginia 22314
(703) 683-9420
http://atra-tr.org

American Network of Community Options and Resources
1101 King Street, Suite 380
Alexandria, Virginia 22314
(703) 535-7850
http://www.ancor.org

Architectural and Transportation Barriers Compliance Board (ATBCB)
1331 F Street, NW, Suite 1000, Washington, DC 20004-1111
(202) 272-5448
(202) 272-5449 (TT)
http://www.access-board.gov

Paul Spicer, QMRP

Association for the Advancement of Rehabilitation Technology (RESNA)
Technical Assistance Project, 1700 North Moore Street, Suite 1540
Arlington, Virginia 22209-1903.
(703) 524-6686
(703) 524-6639 (TTY)
http://www.resna.org

Center for Disability Information & Referral
Indiana Institute on Disability and Community
2853 East Tenth Street
Bloomington, IN 47408-2696
http://www.iidc.indiana.edu

National Alliance of the Disabled
1352 Sioux Street
Orange Park, Florida 32065
http://www.naotd.org/home.html

National Association of Developmental Disabilities Council
1234 Massachusetts Avenue NW, Suite 103
Washington, DC 20005
(202) 347-1234
http://www.naddc.org/

National Clearinghouse for Professionals in Special Education
1920 Association Drive, Reston, Virginia 20191-1589
(800) 641-7824
(703) 264-9480 (TTY)
http://www.specialedcareers.org

National Consortium for Physical Education and Recreation for Individuals with Disabilities
Northern Illinois University
Anderson Hall 236
Dekalb, IL 60115
815-753-1413
http://ncperid.usf.edu/

National Institute on Disability and Rehabilitative Research (NIDRR)
600 Independence Avenue SW, Room 3060 MES
Washington, DC 20202-2572
(202) 205-8134
(202) 205-9136 (TT)
http://www.ed.gov/about/offices/list/osers/nidrr/index.html

National Rehabilitation Information Center (NARIC)
1010 Wayne Avenue, Suite 800
Silver Spring, Maryland 20910-5633
(301) 562-2400
(301) 495-5626 (TTY)
http://www.naric.com.

Office of Civil Rights (OCR)
330 C. Street SW
Washington, DC 20202-1100
(800) 421-3481
(877) 521-2172 (TDD)
http://www.ed.gov/offices/OCR

Office of Special Education and Rehabilitative Services
US Department of Education
400 Maryland Avenue, S.W.
Washington, DC 20202
(202) 205-5465
http://www.ed.gov

President's Committee on Mental Retardation
352 G Hubert Humphrey Building, 200 Independence Avenue
Washington, DC 20202
(202) 619-0634

Spicer & Associates, LLC – Disability Resources, Books, and Workshops
1009 Taylor Avenue
Richmond, Virginia 23225
(804) 405-5231
www.spicerassociates.com
disabilityinfo@spicerassociates.com

ABOUT THE AUTHOR

Paul Spicer, a Qualified Mental Retardation Practitioner, is the author of *Writing Therapy* (Venture Publishing, 2005) and has been invited to speak to the Health Worlds Asia Congress, at the Putra World Trade Center in Malaysia, as well as authored numerous publications and journals on the topic of disabilities and community inclusion.

As the founder and president of Spicer & Associates, Paul has offered disability related workshops and consultancy services in the healthcare arena. His website, www.spice rassociates.com, has served as an online resource for family members and healthcare professionals alike.

Printed in the United States
By Bookmasters